Reclaiming Rural

Reclaiming Rural

Building Thriving
Rural Congregations

Allen T. Stanton

An Alban Institute Book

ROWMAN & LITTLEFIELD
Lanham • Boulder • New York • London

Portions of Chapter 1 were originally published in an essay titled, "Why I Hate Wendell Berry," in *Faith and Leadership* (www.faithandleadership.com), and are used here with permission. The original article can be found at: https://faithandleadership.com/allen-t-stanton-why-i-hate-wendell-berry

Portions of Chapter 2 were previously published in an essay titled "What Churches Can Learn from Higher Education," in *Alban at Duke Divinity*, and are used here with permission. The original article can be found at https://alban.org/2019/11/01/allen-stanton-what-churches-can-learn-from-higher-education/

The indicators of vitality presented in Chapter 2 were originally published in an essay titled "Thriving Rural Congregations" in *Ministry Matters*. They are revised and used here with permission. The original article can be found at: https://www.ministrymatters.com/all/entry/9353/thriving-rural-congregations

Chapter 4 is a revised and expanded version of an article titled "An Economic Community: Rethinking Community Development, Anti-Poverty Work, and Economic Development," first published in Practical Matters 10 (2017) by Emory University. Reproduced here with permission. The original article can be found at: http://practicalmattersjournal.org/2017/04/06/an-economic-community/

Published by Rowman & Littlefield
An imprint of The Rowman & Littlefield Publishing Group, Inc.
4501 Forbes Boulevard, Suite 200, Lanham, Maryland 20706
www.rowman.com

6 Tinworth Street, London SE11 5AL, United Kingdom

British Library Cataloguing in Publication Information Available

Library of Congress Cataloging-in-Publication Data
Names: Stanton, Allen T., 1989- author.
Title: Reclaiming rural : building thriving rural congregations / Allen T. Stanton.
Description: Lanham : Rowman & Littlefield, 2020. | "An Alban Institute Book." | Includes bibliographical references and index. | Summary: "As rural communities continue to undergo massive economic and demographic shifts, rural churches are uniquely positioned to provide community leadership. This book is an energetic and encouraging call for how religious leaders can develop vital church communities in rural America"—Provided by publisher.
Identifiers: LCCN 2020040167 (print) | LCCN 2020040168 (ebook) | ISBN 9781538135235 (cloth) | ISBN 9781538135242 (paperback) | ISBN 9781538135259 (epub)
Subjects: LCSH: Rural churches.
Classification: LCC BV638 .S57 2020 (print) | LCC BV638 (ebook) | DDC 250.9173/4—dc23
LC record available at https://lccn.loc.gov/2020040167
LC ebook record available at https://lccn.loc.gov/2020040168

Contents

Acknowledgments

When I look over the pages of this book, I can see the fingerprints of many, many people. When I was a bit more naive, I thought that writing happened at a desk, alone. And while typing is a solitary activity (and while any remaining mistakes are mine), this book could not be possible without a much wider community.

Laceye Warner and Jeff Conklin-Miller helped, in very direct ways, to give this book life. Before I recognized this as a book project, both tolerated numerous lunches and coffees, offered reading suggestions, and fielded really naive questions. As this project came into focus, Laceye and Jeff read drafts of outlines and chapters, helped me shape my focus, and offered valuable feedback. For some reason, both still answer my texts, e-mails, and phone calls. I appreciate their friendship and mentorship.

Jeremy Troxler introduced me to the creative possibilities of rural ministry, which was nurtured by Kirk Hatherly, David Reeves, and Robb Webb. In particular, Robb has offered a great deal constructive feedback over the years, and my work and vocation are stronger for it.

Meghan Killingsworth, Lynn Taylor, H. G. Stovall, Whitney Mitchell, Timothy Holton, and Melinda Britt are valued conversation partners, colleagues, and friends. I continue to benefit from their creativity, insight, and wisdom. Many of them read drafts of chapters and offered critiques that made these pages stronger. Likewise, Nathan Kirkpatrick and Ken Carter both reminded me that I had something worth saying, and encouraged me to start writing.

I would also be remiss if I didn't acknowledge the support of my colleagues at Martin Methodist College. Shana Hibdon made it possible to find time to write, and over coffee, listened to me think out loud far more than she probably wanted. Domenic Nigrelli asked important questions that helped shape some of my arguments. Mark La Branche offered me my job (I assume against his better judgment), and with it, the chance to do some really fun and meaningful work. The Turner Center's work studies, Tyler Mutter and Leah-Marie Calton, have been able research assistants, and their help is greatly appreciated.

The Thriving Rural Communities Initiative at Duke Divinity School provided valuable study leave for me to write. During that week, my mother-in-law, Pam, was kind enough to help Abby with our child while I was gone, which was greatly appreciated. I'm grateful for Bishop McAlilly and the Tennessee and Memphis Annual Conferences for being willing to see the potential of the rural church, and collaborating to help nurture it.

Merritt's Chapel United Methodist Church was a learning lab for me. They taught me how to pastor, and unwittingly helped me ground many of my theories. This book would not be possible without them.

Finally, I need to thank my own family. Cheryl and Joe Stanton raised my sister, Laura, and me in a small, rural town. It was there that I learned what it meant to be in a community. I hope that I can pass on that sense of community to my own children.

My wife, Abby, is the most encouraging person I have ever met, and constantly shows me how to be a better person. She is a fantastic leader, a wonderful mother, and the best partner I could have asked for. My daughter Paige is teaching me how to be a dad, and reminds me to see the world with wonder and awe. As I write this, we are expecting our second daughter, Natalie, who will be born by the time this book is published. Though we have not met yet, I know she, too, will teach me infinite lessons about life. I hope I am as good a father as they are daughters.

Abby, Paige, and Natalie, this book is for you.

Introduction

During my senior year of college, I felt a call to be ordained, and so I began visiting seminaries. A family friend and adjunct professor at the seminary I eventually attended told me about a scholarship available for incoming students, and he thought I would be a good candidate for it. It did have a catch, though. If I accepted the scholarship, then I would also agree to serve the rural church for at least five years following graduation.

It was not a thrilling prospect for my twenty-two-year-old self. But I was unsure of my vocation. I decided that if I interviewed, I would be taking a faithful step. If the selection committee extended an offer, then that would be a way of discerning my next step. If not, then I could focus on what I wanted to do with my career, which was also unclear.

On a Wednesday afternoon, I received a phone call from the director of the program, letting me know that I had been selected. They would be sending a packet of information, including a covenant that I should sign and return within seven days.

I kept the covenant on my desk and reread it every night for five days. Did I really want to make that commitment? I talked it over with professors, pastors, and friends. The advice, in retrospect, was largely unhelpful. Professors mostly implored me to consider, or not consider, the length of the service commitment. To some, five years was a long time, and I would be a different person after three years of seminary and five years of the rural church. To others, five years would go by quickly. Both of those are true. I am, thankfully, remarkably different than I was at twenty-two, and that time did fly by.

Pastors, likewise, generally fell into two camps. Some advised me to be mindful of my future career. Would serving in the rural church prevent me from climbing whatever sort of pastoral ladder of success? Would that five years be better spent as an associate at a large church? Other pastors reminded me that in my denomination, we are appointed. Most young pastors were appointed to small-membership rural churches, and it just so happens that they stay there for three to five years. If I was going to pursue ordination, I was likely heading to the rural parish, whether I wanted to or not.

My friends, always practical, reminded me of the student loans that I had already accrued and the job security I would have. Of the advice I received, this was the most convincing.

When I look back over that week of discernment, what was most interesting to me was that there were few voices helping me articulate or understand any sort of vocational reason why I would or would not accept such a scholarship with a commitment. No one outside of the scholarship committee asked whether I felt called to the rural church, or whether the rural church had something to teach me.

I accepted the scholarship largely as a means to avoid accruing more student debt, and I decided to live with the ramifications of my decision. At the very least, I would get a great theological education for no cost to me. The rest I could figure out later.

In the first week of class, the director of my program, Jeremy, invited all of the scholarship fellows to a start-of-year dinner. While there, he handed out a map of North Carolina, each county shaded one of three colors. Each color represented one tier of a three-tier economic system, where Tier I counties are the most economically distressed, and Tier III counties are the least.[1] Jeremy pointed out that all of the Tier I counties were rural. Those were, he told us, the communities that we would be serving when we graduated. We were called to those communities, and responding to the needs of those communities would be part of my job.

I hung the map above my desk in my room, where it stayed for the next three years. Here was an opportunity to fuse my passions—for the church, for community development, for public policy—in a real and meaningful way. This was my first step into my vocation with rural communities. It was a vocation that grew and shaped itself throughout seminary, and since seminary. The rural church, I recognized, was a place that could fundamentally transform their communities.

In the years since I hung that map above my desk, I've visited and preached in countless rural congregations, worked in a public policy think tank, pastored a rural congregation, and currently serve at a small rural college, where I support rural congregations as they lead community transformation.

What I've discovered is that the life of the rural community and the rural congregation are necessarily intertwined. This is not surprising. After all, they share a people, a history, and a context. When I attend church now, I see my colleagues, my neighbors, and my friends. This means that, when I go to work, or to the grocery store, or into a local business, I am also seeing my fellow church members. There is no separating my identity between who I am outside of church and who I am inside of church.

That connection extends deeper still, though. Rural churches, like the communities in which they exist, are often misunderstood and maligned. They have, like their communities, adopted false narratives about themselves that prevent them from living into their full potential.

Perhaps the most important potential that rural churches have is to be an anchor institution in their community. Anchor institutions are those community organizations that contribute to the economic and social fabric of the community. These are institutions such as hospitals, universities, businesses, and nonprofits.[2]

In rural America, there are far fewer of these institutions. The college where I serve is the lone four-year college in an eighteen-county radius. We are a small college, with around 1,000 students in total. Comparatively, Nashville, TN, which is about seventy-five minutes north of us, boasts around twenty colleges, including Vanderbilt University.

As one of my colleagues likes to remind anyone who will listen, if one of the colleges in Nashville were to close, another school would quickly take its place in the ecosystem. If our college were to close, we would be losing *the* college that produces nurses, teachers, and entrepreneurs for our region. We would be losing a center of education, jobs, and culture.

The church is a vital anchor institution in rural communities that does not receive enough attention or study. The rural church is one of the rare places where people gather frequently, bringing expertise, passions, and skills in the community. The question that I often ask is, what if we could leverage that for the Kingdom of God?

This book is an attempt to answer that question. It is born out of a passion for rural communities and a pride in the ingenuity and commitment that I see these small-membership churches exhibit. But it is also born out of a deep frustration. A frustration with congregations who have given up their imagination for leading their communities, with church leaders who diminish the potential impact of the overwhelming majority of our congregations,[3] and with theology that does not offer practices for leadership, inadvertently separating theological reflection from practice.

In this book, I want to offer a counternarrative for those who have written off the rural church, while offering a clarifying voice to those who believe the rural church can be more. My central argument is that the rural church can and should establish a practice of evangelism that seeks to recognize, cultivate, announce, and invite the wider community to participate in the Kingdom of God. This practice of evangelism will not only help rural congregations grow in their own faith and discipleship but also position them to be better stewards of their role as anchor institutions, and establish more robust practices of vitality.

To reach this point requires first undoing some of the narratives that surround the rural church, debunking the common assumptions about rural communities and vitality. In chapter 1, I seek to recapture the narrative about rural spaces as a whole. Here, I explore the complex ways that we define the term *rural* and explore two pervasive narratives about rural communities. The first of those is the story of rural communities as an agrarian paradise; the second is the story of rural decay. Ultimately, we see that neither of these is an accurate portrayal of rural America.

In chapter 2, I set out to examine how these narratives shape our understanding of church vitality. We see that these myths closely correspond with perceptions of rural churches, which inadvertently shapes the practices of the rural church, and how we understand vitality. Here, I conclude the chapter by offering three indicators of vitality that the thriving rural church can work toward in their pursuit of being an anchor institution.

Chapter 3 introduces the turn to the theological. Here, I lay out an argument for the practice of evangelism described above. This practice of recognizing, cultivating, announcing, and inviting the community to participate in the Kingdom of God is closely aligned with John Wesley's path of salvation, following the template of prevenient grace, justifying grace, and sanctifying grace. Ultimately, this practice of evangelism seeks to form both the church and the community in practices of faith by offering the community a glimpse of the economic and social realities of the Kingdom of God.

This type of community engagement is not without complications, however. In chapter 4, I explore a few theological tensions that any congregation pursuing such work must come to terms with. First, congregations must explore the tension between charity and justice. Second, they must look at the role of relationships in their community work. Third, they must look at how their theological beliefs are shaping their own motivations for engaging in this work. These are not unnavigable, fortunately.

Any theology of evangelism must be able to be practiced. In chapter 5, I briefly examine three rural congregations whose work exhibits this fourfold template, while exploring some common traits that each of these congregations shared. What we find is that this practice of evangelism allows for growth, creativity, and fosters community leadership.

In the final chapter, I offer a vision for the future of rural church. Ultimately, I believe that the future of the rural church is one that is filled with hope. This does not mean, though, that rural churches can continue without any organizational changes or adjustments to practice.

One of the underlying themes to this book is that there is a great deal of potential for rural congregations, regardless of their size or resources, to participate in the beautiful work that God is already doing. That work is a shared responsibility, among pastors, lay leaders, and denominational leaders.

When writing, I tried to keep all of these audiences in mind. I hope that this book will be helpful to the seminarian who is about to enter into their first rural church pastorate, to the regional denominational official struggling to support the plethora of small congregations they are responsible for, to the pastor of the small church, and to the members of the laity who want to see their congregations seize their potential.

When I entered into seminary, my biggest fear was that I had committed myself to a boring vocation. Having served the rural church, both as a pastor and as a supporter, I am convinced that these churches are full of potential. There need be nothing boring or sleepy about these congregations. They can, in fact, be leaders of dramatic transformation.

NOTES

1. "County Distress Rankings (Tiers)." NC Commerce, 2020, www.nccommerce. com/grants-incentives/county-distress-rankings-tiers.

2. Maurrasse, David. "Anchor Institutions and Their Significance to Community and Economic Development." State of the Planet, March 8, 2016, blogs.ei.columb ia.edu/2016/03/08/anchor-institutions-and-their-significance-to-community-and-ec onomic-development/.

3. Most churches in the United States are small-membership congregations, even as most people attend large congregations. See Chaves, Mark, et al. *Religious Congregations in 21st Century America: National Congregation Study*. National Congregation Study, 2015, 1–57.

Chapter 1

Reclaiming the Narrative

It takes some intentionality to get to the town where I live. Located a bit more than an hour south of Nashville, you still have a fifteen-minute drive into town after you pull off the interstate. The drive is absolutely stunning, though. In the spring, the green rolling hills seem to stretch forever. In the fall, the leaves turn a beautiful mix of orange, amber, and purple. Horses and cows feed beside the road. Tractors prepare their fields for planting. I don't usually mind that there's little cell-phone reception in that stretch; it's fifteen minutes of solitude.

If you had to guess based off that drive, you would assume that agriculture is at the economic and cultural heart of our small community. After all, you'll pass signs for multiple family farms, and almost all of the land on that stretch of road is dedicated to either some crop or livestock. Assuming that we are an agrarian community seems like a safe assumption.

Safe as the assumption might appear, it is almost wholly incorrect. Our largest employers are all manufacturing firms. In my small town, we make headlights that go on Jeeps and Fiats, cookies for Frito-Lay, the rubber that lines the inside of your car's windows, and the signs at the McDonald's drive-through that say, "Order here." We are an industrial community.

About ninety minutes away, in another small community, is an employee-owned company that manufactured the flagpole Neil Armstrong and Buzz Aldrin placed on the moon. A frequent contractor for NASA, they are the engineers behind the fastest man-made craft ever flown.

When I hold up this alternative narrative of rural places, I'm usually told that these communities "aren't your typical rural community." Which raises inevitable questions: What is the typical rural community? Is there even such a thing?

When I began my ministry, I was told time and time again that I needed to know and understand my community. Like many of my colleagues, I began my tenure visiting with my parishioners, listening to their stories. I heard stories of families torn apart by drugs, of retired professors from prestigious programs, of family tension, of hopes and dreams, honored traditions, and suffocating routines.

Those stories were vitally important to my parish ministry. They gave me insight into how to lead my church, helping me understand the pain points where it was best to apply pressure, and where I needed to let a situation resolve on its own. They helped me understand when a tense meeting was a moment of pastoral care, and when managed conflict was necessary for spiritual and organizational growth. These stories gave me language to understand and communicate our values so that we could all articulate our next steps in our journey of discipleship. They pointed to a vision for the congregation that was rooted in our natural gifts.

The stories of our communities are vitally important. No quality pastor would walk into a parish and assume that they understand the rhythms of that congregational life. And yet, rural pastors and their denominational leaders often enter into their communities armed *only* with assumptions of what life in a rural community entails.

I suspect these assumptions are rooted in right intentions. A pastor might have grown up in a different rural community, and so they form an assumption based on their prior lives. Or a pastor might have earnestly read stories in national newspapers, attempting to understand the challenges facing their new community. Nevertheless, assumptions are almost always flawed.

When people describe rural communities, they tend to offer one of two narratives. The first is popular within theological circles, placing an emphasis on agrarianism, often using the terms "agrarian" and "rural" interchangeably. Such a narrative is useful for certain theological arguments, bolstering the importance of creation and community.

The second narrative, and perhaps the more popular of the two, paints rural communities as places of inevitable decline. Propelled by books like JD Vance's *Hillbilly Elegy*, these narratives skew data to show that rural communities will inevitably collapse.

While there are bits of truth in both of those narratives, neither can realistically claim to offer a definitive picture of rural, and both fail to engage with the nuance of rural places. The majority of this chapter will be spent analyzing and offering some corrections to these narratives. First, though, it is important to consider how we define what a rural community is.

WHAT IS RURAL?

Whenever I talk with groups about rural communities, I like to start with a two-question quiz. First, I ask my audience to define *urban*. Groups tend to work this through fairly logically: a city is a place with lots of people. So once a place has a high enough population, it's considered urban, they reason. It's fairly sound logic. The U.S. Census Bureau defines an urban area as a place with a population of more than 50,000.

The second question seems just as simple: Can you define *rural*? Here, the guesses get wilder, as the audience tries to uncover a simple definition. Maybe, they reason, it's any place that's not urban. But that would include a huge number of suburbs, tucked right outside of cities, or in between cities. Some guess a population threshold (like less than 10,000 people) or population density (less than 250 people per square mile). A few usually make a cultural definition: a rural community is a place with cows, with Dollar Generals, or places that are at least 45 miles from a Target or Walmart.

None of these definitions really work, though. While urban communities can be easily identified, rural communities exist as a spectrum. Definitions of rural capture snapshots, rather than painting a whole portrait, in large part because a whole portrait is nearly impossible to capture.

As a colleague of mine likes to say, "When you've seen one rural community, you've seen exactly one rural community."

Consider three very different rural counties in the United States. Clay County, North Carolina, is nestled in the Appalachian Mountains, on the North Carolina—Georgia State Line. The entire county has a population of less than 11,000. The largest town, Hayesville, only boasts a population of around 400. In recent years, the county has become something of a hot-spot for retiring baby boomers. Locals call them half-backs: they moved from the north to Florida, discovered it was too hot, and so they moved halfway back, settling in the mountains of NC. Lake Chatuge, a Tennessee Valley Authority lake, offers stunning views and a recreational center for the region. Because of the natural amenities—mountains, a lake, and a river—it is little wonder that property prices have begun to climb.

Davison County, South Dakota, is spectacularly different from Hayesville. Its largest attraction is the Corn Palace, which welcomes 200,000 to 500,000 visitors each year. The Corn Palace is decorated with thirteen different shades of corn to create murals and artwork that are updated each year. The county is also the home of Dakota Wesleyan University, whose basketball team plays in the Corn Palace. The university itself has just under 1,000 students in its myriad of undergraduate and 3 graduate degree programs. Rather than mountains, lakes, and rivers, the Davison County landscape boasts farmlands stretching for miles.

Monroe County, Florida, is flat, but whereas Davison County has rows of fields, Monroe County is a mixture of sandy beaches and wetlands. The majority of the county is made up of the virtually uninhabited Everglades, while 99 percent of the almost 77,000 residents live in the more hospitable islands of the Florida Keys. Key West, Florida, the county seat, has a population double that of Clay and Davison Counties, and is heavily dependent upon tourism and seasonal guests.

These three counties have very little in common—they have very different economic drivers, they have little in common culturally, and geographically, they could not be more disparate. Yet, they are all rural, at least according to a frequently used definition within the U.S. Department of Agriculture (USDA).

Establishing exactly what constitutes rural is exceedingly difficult. There are rural communities that look, feel, and behave like suburban communities (not to mention suburban areas that feel rural in nature). And there are rural communities that are far removed from any metropolitan area. So, where do rural communities start and urban, suburban, and exurban communities end?

There is no simple answer for that question, and there never has been. In 1938, W. H. Meserole wrote an essay in which he stated one cannot simply draw a line to mark what is rural and urban. Rather, he wrote, "the transit from rural to urban—or from urban to rural, if you prefer, is a shading process. One imperceptibly melds into the other."[1] If this was already a reality in 1938, consider how much truer this is in contemporary times, when geographic mobility has become normative.

Rather than a single demarcation, people have adopted a wide variety of definitions. Some look at the population of a county, looking at population totals or population density. Such definitions, however, risk leaving out large swaths of rural communities in predominantly urban counties.

One popular definition, used by the U.S. Department of Agriculture's Economic Research Service, defines rural based on commuting patterns. The Rural–Urban Commuting Area (RUCA) codes look at every U.S. Census tract in the United States—which in some cases is quite a small geographic area—and assigns it a code that corresponds to that area's commuting flow to nearby urban areas. Those census tracts that have a code of 1–3 are considered urban. Those with a code of 4–10 are considered rural.

This definition is useful for three major reasons. First, it can be updated with every census. Second, it is more granular, and so communities that might be in an urban county are included. Third, it is not tied to an arbitrary number, which may eventually fall out of use. For example, the Duke Endowment, a philanthropy in North Carolina that focuses in part on rural community development, originally used a definition of rural as any community with less than 1,500 people. When this definition was written in the organization's Indenture of Trust, it was exceedingly generous. Today, it would prevent the majority of rural communities in North Carolina from funding eligibility. To counteract that, the Duke Endowment adopted RUCA codes as their definition of rural.

While useful, such a definition is not without flaws. Census tracts do not follow community boundaries, and so a community can potentially be split into two different tracts. The road in front of my former parish was a census tract boundary. The side of the street where my church was located was considered to be part of an urbanized core. Across the street, it was considered to be rural. There was no real difference—culturally or economically—between the people who lived next door to the church and the people who lived across the street from us. So was my church rural or urban?

Why does any of this matter? At first glance, deciding what is and what's not a rural community may feel like an academic exercise. One might assume that any of the myriad of definitions measures essentially the same thing, encompassing essentially the same geographic area, with minor squabbles about communities where we need to draw a clear marker between rural and urban. According to the USDA, depending on the definition one uses, the share of the U.S. population that can be classified as rural can range anywhere from 17 percent to 49 percent.[2]

That the population of rural America can fluctuate by such a large margin should give us pause when we begin to reflect on the narratives surrounding rural communities. When we read national stories about rural decline, are we talking about less than one-fifth of the population, or are we talking about nearly half? When we describe rural communities and their people through cultural terms—uneducated, farmers, aging, isolated, and tight-knit—who are we trying to describe?

Given the inability to create a single, static definition of rural politically, culturally, or sociologically, it is somewhat surprising that we tend to discuss rural communities in rather uncomplicated terms.

Faced with the impossibility of describing a wide and diverse number of communities, rural communities are instead described in monolithic terms, usually falling into one of two national narratives. These simple narratives embrace generalities and stereotypes, rather than explore the nuance of rural communities.

The first narrative is one rooted in a romantic view of agrarianism. The second is one that views rural as synonymous with decline. These prevailing narratives are damaging not just for the people who live outside of rural communities, who speak about rural culture broadly and flippantly. They also do damage to the people who live within communities. In some cases, they shape national policies. But they also shape the internal narrative that communities use to characterize themselves. Too often, they prevent the very real gifts and challenges of rural places from being witnessed.

AGRARIAN PARADISE

During my final year of seminary, I sat in a professor's office to talk about political theology in rural communities. The professor predicated his work on a theological model of the City, firmly rooted in Augustine's theology. My question was about how it might translate to rural areas. My professor's answer was that it was well suited for agrarian political theology and that the basics of a community were the same, whether it was urban or not.

I pointed out that a significant portion of the rural communities around our school were dependent upon manufacturing. What does a rural, nonagrarian, political theology look like?

"Even if people aren't farmers," he answered, "the retail and manufacturing in rural areas goes to support farming."

Brilliant theologian though he was, my professor was sorely mistaken about the realities of rural communities. In his mind, as in the minds of many, rural communities are synonymous with agriculture.

It is an unsurprising assumption. After all, a drive through the country will showcase field after field of crops and livestock. Mines, factories, and hospitals might offer more jobs, but their footprint is significantly smaller.

To be fair, for most of the United States' history, the terms *rural* and *agrarian* could in fact be used interchangeably. As recently as the conclusion of World War II, more than half of rural Americans were farmers. Most of those relied upon their farms for their livelihoods. By the new millennium, farmers only accounted for 7 percent of the rural population. Of that, 57 percent of the farmers are hobbyists, producing crops and livestock for their own use or to sell at farmers' markets.[3] Today, most rural communities would not be classified as "farming-dependent." In 2015, only 391 counties—about 19.7 percent of all nonmetropolitan counties—were considered farm-dependent. For comparison, manufacturing-dependent counties accounted for 348, or 17.6 percent, of nonmetropolitan counties.

When people talk about agrarian communities, they are assuming more than just economics, though. More often, and particularly within theological circles, they are presuming cultural markers that might or might not exist. Consider the prevailing theological writer on agrarianism: Wendell Berry.

In ministry, Wendell Berry is ubiquitous. In rural ministry, he is inescapable. He is quoted in conference presentations and referenced in sermons. His poems are read as *lectio divina* at retreats. He is the subject of documentaries, and you can even find an album of his poems arranged for a choral group.

I grew up in a rural community, the kind you would read about in one of Berry's novels. During the summer, I would wake up early and ride with my mom, a schoolteacher, to my great-aunt's house. We would pick corn, green beans, butter beans, and potatoes in her garden. The garden itself was several acres of land, comprised of a mixture of my relatives' land and my great-uncle's brother.

During the school year, I would walk with my older sister to the elementary school a few blocks away. After school, I would congregate with the rest of the neighborhood kids at one of their houses, or wander in and out of the local shops on main street.

In high school, I worked at one of those shops. It was a small family-owned grocery store, and from the time I could read, I knew that I would one day work there after school. I stocked shelves, bagged groceries, and carried bags out for our customers—people I knew by name. The owner, the assistant manager, the butcher, and the baker had all, quite literally, known me since birth.

Church was a central part of the community, and most people either went to the Baptist church (my family), or the local United Methodist church. In my small-membership church, I was encouraged from a young age to take leadership responsibilities, sit on committees, and have an active voice. I was mentored by older congregation members.

My town was a place of safety and stability, filled with people I knew and loved, and who knew and- loved me. When I completed my Eagle Scout project, the local newspaper placed my photo on the front page—above the fold—and dropped off a large stack of papers on our door, free of charge. The community was central to my identity, and the people of the town all had a hand in shaping and forming me.

On the surface, the entire community was a picturesque embodiment of Wendell Berry's ideal community. When I ask people to describe an imagined rural community, they often produce a snapshot like the one I described, naming the supposed qualities that people value about rural places: a tight-knit community, safety, quiet, and quaintness.

In *Jayber Crow*, Berry offers a similar description of the fictional town of Port William. Port William is not a flourishing town, but this is easily glossed over, as Berry focuses the reader's attention on the ethos of the community. People in the Depression Era town have a commitment to the small businesses that populate main street, prioritizing the economic community.[4]

Berry produces an idealized description of an agrarian community, extolling particular values. The community as described in *Jayber Crow* is aspirational in nature. Berry hopes that these values will inspire and be adopted by readers. It is literature designed to elicit a reflection upon our own society, and offer an alternative moral vision.

Berry's writing, in which an agrarian community demonstrates superior morality, is familiar. Like the assumption that "rural" and "agrarian" are interchangeable, the idea that agrarian communities offer a deep morality is rooted in the history of the United States, and in fact intertwined with a unique sense of patriotism.

Borrowing from earlier Greek writers, Enlightenment philosophy fused with the needs of the early American Republic. In this new country, farmers represented self-sustenance, a symbol of independence from Britain. As David Danbom notes, farmers represented everything the British monarchy was not: simple, thrifty, and hardworking. As such, they quickly became the ideal American patriot. For those with property, ownership of the land represented a symbol of their investment in the new republic. Quite literally, farmers owned a stake of this democracy.[5]

This American ideal found itself recapitulated in literature. Henry David Thoreau emphasized simplicity, connection to the land, and independence in his book *Walden*. Ralph Waldo Emerson and Henry Wadsworth Longfellow likewise wrote fondly of their appreciation of nature, imbuing it with a purer morality. In doing so, rurality came to represent virtuousness.

It is in this line of thought that Berry's work stands, a commentary on what rural communities *might* offer. It should be said that Berry is not ignorant of the hardships facing rural America, particularly those communities that are agrarian. He is a keen observer of rural challenges. He ably diagnosis the problems, even if his prescription is to return to agrarianism.

The issue here is not that Wendell Berry, Thomas Jefferson, or Thoreau idealize agrarianism, but that such writings are extracted to real rural communities by their readers. Rather than remain aspirational, pastors often use Berry as proof of what they believe to be an existing rural landscape. When large, tall steeple pastors quote Wendell Berry to rural pastors to emphasize the importance of rural ministry, the aspirational morality is assumed to already exist. Rather than using Berry as a point to deepen their understanding of rural places, such readers instead flatten the community into the ideal.

Consider an essay by *New York Times* columnist David Brooks, entitled "What Rural America has to Teach Us." Brooks begins by remarking on the "moral coherence and social commitment" that rural communities have.[6] He goes on to describe various anecdotes to demonstrate this superior morality: people leaving their cars unlocked, high civic participation, and a general sense of trust in the community.

Though he does not cite Berry as an inspiration, Brooks draws deeply in this vein, writing, "Farm life inculcates an insane work ethic, which gets carried into community life." While his essay is about a specific community in Nebraska, a farm heavy state, Brooks extrapolates his observations to rural communities everywhere. In doing so, he reinforces the narrative that rural, agrarian communities are idyllic and intrinsically virtuous.

It is certainly not bad to emphasize the positive qualities of communities. When I talk about the town in which I live, I mention the low crime rate, the helpfulness of my neighbors, and the strong support system in place.

There is also a danger in overemphasizing these qualities. Such idealization allows people to disengage from realities facing a community. I can easily gloss over the impending shift in manufacturing that will eliminate half of the jobs in my community, or that, when I walk with my daughter to church, we pass by the building in which the Ku Klux Klan was founded.

Perhaps even more dangerous, such idealization allows people to disengage from the realities facing rural communities and begin to commodify them. Notice the title assigned to David Brooks' essay: "Rural America" is decidedly separate from "Us." The value of the rural community is not the way in which rural and urban communities are interconnected, but rather in what rural communities can offer—in this case, a lesson in morality.

When my urban counterparts quote Wendell Berry to me, or talk about the deep morality that exists in agrarian communities, they often do so in a way that reinforces this commodification. Rural places are picturesque and simple, as opposed to the complex and harried pace of the city. Urban leaders might enjoy them at a distance, but they are not places in which to serve, live, or work.

This idealism allows my urban colleagues to disengage from rural spaces, giving them permission to ignore the ways our communities are interconnected. It allows people to believe that rural churches and communities have nothing to teach except as a nostalgic model. That oversimplification allows leaders in government, in business, and even in our denominations to offer one-size solutions that fail to take seriously the complexity of our rural places.

And, this idealism leads to another faulty assumption: if rural communities are morally superior, then there is nothing that needs to be done support them. Rural communities become places of fantasy. Fantasy cannot restore, because it refuses to see what is real. Our rural communities deserve better than romantic images.

RURAL DECAY

After Donald Trump's surprising election in 2016, rural communities found themselves thrust into the national conversation as people tried to understand the distinctive social, economic, and political concerns of rural America. In the aftermath of the 2016 election, J. D. Vance's memoir *Hillbilly Elegy: A Memoir of a Family and Culture in Crisis* became a map, used to understand how rural America was so pivotal in the election.

Vance's book is not the only, nor the first, of its kind. Vance's hypothesis is clear: rural America is dying because rural communities embrace a "a culture that encourages social decay instead of counteracting it."[7] In rural communities, this hypothesis suggests, people are angry, and their anger leads them to advocate for and perpetuate government systems that damage the community. Vance writes from a decidedly conservative political position. Rural people do not need government support; it only further decays the culture. As proof, Vance offers his own life—he escaped rural America, pulled himself by his bootstraps, attended law school at Yale, and became a venture capitalist.

While fundamentally conservative in nature, *Hillbilly Elegy* also fits a decidedly progressive narrative about rural, wherein rural communities are uncultured, egregiously conservative on social and political issues to the point of self-destruction, and they are therefore in a precipitous decline. Effectively, Vance furthers the narrative that rural communities, who elected Donald Trump, are the ones inhibiting meaningful social change.

Importantly, *Hillbilly Elegy* is not intended to be a book about rural America at large. It is instead a book about Appalachia, itself a large and diverse region encompassing both rural and urban areas. Yet, the narrative of decline and decay contained within it is extrapolated to every rural community.

Equally as important is the fact that, while the narrative of an agrarian paradise is cultural and values-based, Vance's argument is both cultural and economic. The economic failings of rural America are due to cultural failings in those communities.

In a way, Vance's work becomes a useful litmus test. As discussions about the rural–urban divide became more common following Trump's election, *Hillbilly Elegy* was often invoked by people who had little experience with rural areas. Vance allowed them to claim a new understanding of rural communities, without having to interact with them.

Urban America's fascination with *Hillbilly Elegy* points toward a deeper issue of class. T. R. C Hutton points out that Vance's work stands in a long line of literature about poor, rural whites, a literary genre dating back at least to Samuel Clemens.[8] In locating Vance in this long chain of literature about rural America, readers find that the common diagnosis is that rural communities – where "rural," "poor," and "white" are wrongly interchangeable—are poor because they failed to emulate the cultural norms of the more elite citizens.

Hillbilly Elegy continues this narrative. Throughout the book, Vance offers a bifurcated identity, clearly distinguishing life in his hometown in Ohio and his time at Yale. At one point, Vance notices that the cultural norms at Yale, a place of success, were vastly different than his culture in Ohio. He tells a story about the only time he took a Yale-friend to eat at Cracker Barrell. A favorite restaurant during Vance's teenage years, it is regarded by his friends as greasy and unhealthy. In the experience, Vance recognizes that he is a "cultural alien." Rather than defend his Appalachian culture, Vance begins to question the difference of culture, asking, "Why are people like me so poorly represented in America's elite institutions?" and "Why did successful people feel so different?"[9]

One might focus on any number of systemic issues—extraction economies, shifting labor forces, and lack of infrastructure in some communities. Vance answers those questions in the subtitle of his book, where he describes "a culture in crisis." The implication, of course, is that successful people abandon the culture of their rural places in order to become successful.

While I did not attend an Ivy League school, I did attend an elite, nationally ranked private university for my undergraduate work. Many of my classmates were substantially wealthier than my own family, which was solidly middle class. I learned fairly quickly that those parts of my story that linked me to my rural community were to be hidden.

Early in my freshman year, my classmates and I sat in the formal dining room discussing our future aspirations over lunch. We went around the table and shared what we wanted to do after graduation. For most of us, it was law school, finance, or medical school.

One of my classmates said that she wanted to apply for Teach for America. I was not fully aware what Teach for America was, but I knew that my favorite teachers in high school were part of that program. I complimented her on the decision, telling her about my high school biology teacher, who had just entered a prestigious medical school.

Quietly, my classmate explained to me that Teach for America is a program that places recent college graduates in the most impoverished and lowest-performing schools in the United States. Without knowing it, I had confessed that my high school was inadequate, underperforming, and underfunded. Then, my classmate exploded.

"I went to one of the most prestigious prep schools in the America," she told me. "You went to a poor, rural high school in the middle of nowhere. It makes me mad that people like you get to come here."

The lesson I learned was a hard one: do not reveal my rural background. No one celebrated that my high school biology teacher fostered an appreciation for a subject that I generally disdained, or that I performed well enough on the SAT, despite not having access to the same expensive SAT tutors as my wealthier classmates. No one acknowledged the exceptional teachers that created independent studies to help me become a better writer, which enabled me to place out of the required freshman writing seminar. Rather, the rural background was a mark against me and my future success.

Most of this elitism is not so obvious; generally, it is much subtler. When my wife and I moved to our current location, where we live in a beautifully renovated historical home that we could not have afforded in our previous city, well-intentioned urbanites often shared tips for living in rural communities. "You're close enough to the city," I hear often, "that you can go to get out here when you need to. Just for a weekend. I know I would need a weekend in the city every now and then." Such advice tends to not consider that people might prefer rural communities, even as Gallup polls regularly show that people do in fact prefer to live in rural places.[10]

Such urban elitism is prevalent throughout Vance's book, and it serves as a salve to readers who can quickly highlight the ailments of rural America without considering their own community's societal problems. Elizabeth Catte, an historian of Appalachia, writes about her interactions with wealthy Texans shortly after *Hillbilly Elegy*'s release:

> It's a strange experience to be grilled about the social decline of "your people" less than five hundred yards from a refinery that gives poor African Americans cancer, but that is what happened to us. At the local university, people whose wall art had been eaten by pollution were suddenly and deeply fascinated by the tragedies of Appalachia.[11]

The narrative of rural decline allows rural communities to be other-ized in ways that defend an elite culture. The problem, though, is that the prevailing narrative of failing rural communities is not accurate.

Rather than testing this narrative of decline against the data, national conversations have largely relied upon the narrative of decline to shape how data is interpreted. Or, more accurately, which data is examined and which data is ignored.

In December 2018, the *New York Times* published an online analytical article entitled, "The Hard Truths of Trying to 'Save' the Rural Economy."[12] Predictably, the piece explores whether or not rural communities can recover from their supposed decline. It is also predictably steeped in political concerns, rather than economic ones: the 2016 election, the author says, brought "the troubles of small-town America to national attention."

The piece begins with the assumption that rural communities are in a state of decline and pushes datasets to prove that assumption. This type of data is not all that hard to find. Writing in a similar vein, David Swenson, an economist at Iowa State University, mapped the population of rural communities and determined that more than half showed no population growth between 2008 and 2017.[13]

To be sure, these types of articles highlight important challenges facing many rural communities in America. What they do not do, though, is tell the whole story of rural America. For instance, consider the prevailing narrative of population decline. If you took the population of rural counties in 1974 and measured their growth, you would find that those rural communities tripled in population.[14]

Some rural communities grew so much that they are no longer classified as rural communities. As rural communities grow, the increase in population eventually necessitates that they stop being called "rural."

Contemporary analysis rarely looks at that growth or considers that when reporting on the health of a community. Historically, rural communities tend to be desirable places to live. A 2018 Gallup survey reported that the largest segment of those polled desired to live in a rural community, more than double the amount that reported wanting to live in a large city.[15] As people move into these communities, they eventually outgrow the rural designation.

To paraphrase a metaphor from Andy Isserman, the popular narrative that speaks only of rural decline without recognizing that rural places are historically desirable is like sending the best college players from a single team to a professional league each year. Eventually, only the worst players are left.

There are numerous studies that speak to the vibrancy of life found in rural communities, and indeed in rural culture itself. In an age of inequality, rural areas can teach urban ones an important lesson, as multiple studies have shown that rural communities have a greater potential for economic mobility than metropolitan areas, due in part to stronger social ties and larger families.[16]

Along with the narrative of decline, rural communities are often described as white and poor. And yet, these assumptions often do injustice to the complexities of rural communities. They do, however, bolster arguments in our national political conversation. Rural states, typically more conservative, are deemed monolithically white. In some cases, this is true. In Appalachia, where *Hillbilly Elegy* is set, the population is predominately white. But, as Catte notes, the African American population in Appalachia is growing at a faster rate than most of the nation.[17] And the largest populations of Native Americans and African Americans are mostly located in predominately rural states.[18]

It is also not true that rural necessarily equates to poverty. The poet Elizabeth Hadaway writes of an experience when a favorite author compliments her poetry in a magazine interview, describing her as "poor and white, from Appalachia." Hadaway points out that her book of poetry, which is about being from Appalachia, never references poverty. She does not claim to be from poverty, but points out that school trips and extra lessons for her sport were luxuries for her, even if they might be standard among her suburban counterparts.[19]

The false equivalency, Hadaway rightly highlights, is not necessarily an insult, even if it can be used as one (and often is). The assumption that everyone in rural communities is poor is also a dangerous one. It hides, for instance, the old money that frequently runs in rural communities, and tends to gloss over the sharp distinctions between those who are impoverished and those who are not.

Hutton notes that J. D. Vance wrote his book not for the people of his hometown, but rather for more highly educated populations.[20] The narrative offers a salve that eliminates systemic issues of poverty in rural communities—for example, the plight of contract chicken farmers, coal miners, and spotty access to broadband and cellular networks—and instead allows populations to believe that poverty in rural America is due to a cultural backwardness. It is a view that is appealing to both conservatives who believe in self-destiny and limited government, and to socially progressive people who see rural communities as the villains of national politics.

None of this is meant to paint a false and rosy picture of rural communities. To do so would be to revert to the moral superiority of the Agrarian Paradise. It is unarguable that rural communities have unique challenges. There are higher rates of poverty, access to broadband is limited, rural hospitals are closing at alarming rates, and automation will eliminate an enormous number of jobs in the coming decades.

Rather, I want to suggest that these challenges differ from community to community. Just as one can pull a short list of urban areas that are in sharp decline, one can easily identify unique challenges that exist in individual communities. It is simply not true, though, that rural communities are wholesale declining and dying.

COEXISTING NARRATIVES

At first glance, these two narratives seem largely incompatible with one another, and yet they are often placed side by side. J. D. Vance explains the culture failings of rural communities, leading to their economic decline, while Wendell Berry, Thomas Jefferson, and Henry David Thoreau confirm the moral superiority found within them. How can both of these narratives coexist?

In large part, they are able to coexist because of the formation of social memory. The noted sociologist Paul Connerton writes that social memory forms through formal and informal commemorative actions.[21] The dominant commemorations of success—graduating from a prestigious university, accents and language, and clothing—are shaped by predominantly urban and suburban cultures. Meanwhile, the dominant social narrative of American values *is* one that is easily identified in agrarian cultures, perpetuating values such as hard work, humility, and strong community ties.

When I graduated from high school, a close family friend chided me for attending an expensive private college rather than a more affordable state school. They pointed out, correctly, that many people in my community had attended the regional school, and they had received a fine education for a much more affordable price. They reminded me that the culture of the elite private school would be substantially different than the community in which I grew up. I would be better off, they told me, by attending the more affordable school, where I would better appreciate and return to the community that raised me. Plus, they concluded pithily, I, "ought not to get too big for my britches."

Their argument highlights the differences of these narratives. You might consider the appeal to uphold the agrarian values. Our family friend asked me to embrace my rural roots, to come back when I had graduated and contribute to the community that raised me. They asked me to prudently consider the financial burden that I would place on myself if I went to the more expensive school. And they pointed out the culture of the community itself, asking me to remember the values in which I had been formed. All of these are values invoked in the narrative of the agrarian paradise—a link to community, a necessary social utilitarianism, humility, and a commitment to the ethics of the community.

The same advice can also be heard as discouragement. Rather than encourage me to attend the best school I could attend, my parents' friend was trying to convince me that I should not invest in my education, and instead attend a less prestigious institution. Encouraging me to return to my hometown was a feeble attempt at reducing brain drain—the phenomenon of college-educated young adults leaving rural communities—which would actively prevent me from exploring other opportunities. In this view, our family friend's advice was an embrace of a failing culture that did not want success.

In competition here are these two dominant narratives. The characterization of success exemplified in J. D. Vance's work is formed in urban and suburban cultures, which do in fact hold more wealth than rural communities (even as the cost of living is more affordable in rural places). Speech and behavior that do not reflect those urban and suburban habits are interpreted as proof that rural communities do not value success. If they did, they would adapt their culture, industry, and lifestyle to accommodate urban influence. This is particularly true as fewer and fewer people are employed in traditionally rural jobs. Misapplied statistics are used to bolster this narrative rather than correct it.

At the same time, the history of agrarian communities in the United States offered a community ethic that was deeply intertwined with our stated national values and even our theological values. When we reference those values, we tend to create an idealized perception of rural communities. Without noting the significant economic and cultural change taking place in these areas, we commodify rural communities, making them contrived realities of our ideals, without ever wanting to live in or linger in them.

RURAL RECKONING

If neither of the two popular narratives surrounding rural communities is accurate, is there one that is?

The short answer is no. In the United States, rural communities are immensely diverse, and globally even more so. To speak about a singular rural narrative is to flatten the distinctive differences in each community, differences that provide an abundance of assets, possibilities, and challenges that require responses. One can speak about national trends, but the local stories of each community will tell a more accurate, complex, and beautiful story.

Rather than attempt a new narrative, I want to instead offer a few observations about the rural communities. First, as I have tried to emphasize throughout this chapter, it is inappropriate to portray rural communities as wholly in decline or wholly vital. To be sure, there are some rural communities with a staggering number of challenges. Hospitals continue to close in rural communities at alarming rates, exacerbating challenges with access to quality care. Likewise, many rural communities are facing tremendous population decline, and the automation of many rural jobs will have a profound impact on the jobs that remain solidly rural.

At the same time, there are many rural communities that are thriving. As retirees move away from urban cores in search of natural amenities and affordable lifestyles, rural communities are in high demand. And, many rural communities have thriving industries that are deeply connected to the region around them.

Second, there is no such thing as a stereotypical rural community. The term "rural" is tossed around as shorthand for a variety of descriptors. But, no two rural communities are exactly alike. Throughout the United States, rural communities fall along a broad scope. They might be described as any number of community types: retirement villages, industrial communities, tourist destinations—the list is endless. It does little good to try to pinpoint a singular description or definition, and it does significantly more harm than good to generalize about rural communities writ large.

This brings me to my third and final observation. As leaders in the church, either lay or clergy, we are tasked with serving the communities in which our churches are found. More often than not, we begin our ministry in our communities with assumptions, rather than a deep understanding of the particularities of our communities. One would not move from New York City to Houston and expect the same culture; neither should we move from one rural community to another without taking the time to understand the story of the community in which we are placed.

More often than not, it will be a story that does not neatly fall into either of the narratives described here. It will, instead, be a story that borrows deeply from both, with urgent needs and unexpected gifts.

NOTES

1. Meserole, W. H. "What Do You Mean: Rural and Urban?" *Journal of Marketing* 2, no. 3 (January 1938). doi:10.2307/1246386.

2. Cromartie, John, and Shawn Bucholtz. "Defining the 'Rural' in Rural America." *USDA ERS*. June 1, 2008. Accessed May 22, 2019, https://www.ers.usda .gov/amber-waves/2008/june/defining-the-rural-in-rural-america/.

3. Danbom, David B. *Born in the Country: A History of Rural America*. 3rd ed. Baltimore, MD: Johns Hopkins University Press, 2017.

4. Berry, Wendell. *Jayber Crow: The Life Story of Jayber Crow, Barber, of the Port William Membership, as Written by Himself*. Thorndike, ME: Thorndike Press, 2001.

5. Danbom, *Born in the Country*, 61–62.

6. Brooks, David. "What Rural America Has to Teach Us." *The New York Times*. March 21, 2019. Accessed May 29, 2019, https://www.nytimes.com/2019/03/21/ opinion/nebraska-rural-america.html.

7. Vance, J. D. *Hillbilly Elegy: A Memoir of a Family and Culture in Crisis*. New York, NY: Harper, an Imprint of HarperCollins Publishers, 2018. 7.

8. Hutton, T. R. C. "Hillbilly Elitism." In *Appalachian Reckoning: A Region Responds to Hllbilly Elegy*, 21–33. Morgantown, WV: West Virginia University Press, 2019.

9. Vance, *Hillbilly Elegy*, 205–7.

10. Newport, Frank. "Americans Big on Idea of Living in the Country." *Gallup.com*, September 4, 2019, news.gallup.com/poll/245249/americans-big-idea-living-country.aspx.

11. Catte, Elizabeth. *What You Are Getting Wrong About Appalachia*. Independent Pub Group, 2018. 8.

12. Porter, Eduardo. "The Hard Truths of Trying to 'Save' the Rural Economy." *The New York Times*. December 14, 2018. Accessed May 29, 2019, https://www.nyt imes.com/interactive/2018/12/14/opinion/rural-america-trump-decline.html.

13. Swenson, David. "Most of America's Rural Areas Are Doomed to Decline." *The Conversation*. May 21, 2019. Accessed May 29, 2019, https://theconversation.c om/most-of-americas-rural-areas-are-doomed-to-decline-115343?utm_medium=ema il&utm_campaign.

14. Goetz, Stephan J., Mark D. Partridge, and Heather M. Stephens. "The Economic Status of Rural America in the President Trump Era and beyond." *Applied Economic Perspectives and Policy* 40, no. 1 (2018): 97–118. doi:10.1093/aepp/ppx061.

15. Gallup, Inc. "Americans Big on Idea of Living in the Country." *Gallup.co m*. Accessed June 7, 2019, https://news.gallup.com/poll/245249/americans-big-idea-living-country.aspx.

16. One such study is Weber, Bruce, J. Matthew Fannin, Kathleen Miller, and Stephan Goetz. "Intergenerational Mobility of Low-income Youth in Metropolitan and Non-metropolitan America: A Spatial Analysis." *Regional Science Policy & Practice* 10, no. 2 (2018): 87–101. doi:10.1111/rsp3.12122.

17. Ibid., 14.

18. According to the 2010 U.S. Census.

19. Hadway, Elizabeth. "Poet, Priest, and 'Poor White Trash.'" In *Appalachian Reckoning*, 390–400. Morgantown, WV: West Virginia University Press, 2019. 395–96.

20. Hutton, "Hillbilly Elitism," 23.

21. Connerton, Paul. *How Societies Remember*. Cambridge: Cambridge University Press, 1989.

Chapter 2

Reclaiming Vitality

In the first chapter, I outlined two competing narratives of rural communities. The first, the story of the *Agrarian Paradise*, views rural communities as places of deep morality, steeped in communitarianism. The second, the narrative of *Rural Decay*, posits that there is something intrinsically wrong with rural communities that causes them to fail.

These narratives are sustained by the way that social memory is formed. Rural places have become the stand-in for the values that we as a culture strive to uphold, chiefly: humility, community, perseverance, and hard work. Urban and suburban places reflect our notions of success, including growth and wealth.

It will come as no surprise that these narratives and their values permeate the way that we think about rural church leadership. In the first narrative, rural churches are places where the task is pure and simple: a pastor who loves the members of the congregation, and parishioners who care for each other, reminding us of why we found our way to the church or to ministry in the first place. In the second narrative, rural churches are places of failure. With dwindling populations, their best days are well into their past. Their buildings, in some cases, are literally decaying, and they are either devoid of quality leadership or they are not trying the right church growth techniques.

Neither of these narratives accurately captures the diversity of rural communities. Some rural congregations are places of deep community and represent the best of our faith. Others are toxic systems, dominated by a few bullies. Some churches are destined to die, and it is our duty to help them die well. Some churches have been presented as terminal when the diagnostic tools are far from accurate. Some are thriving and vital, despite expectations.

If we are to help more rural churches and their communities thrive, we need to be able navigate the ways these narratives have conditioned us to

view rural congregations, so that we might offer indicators of vitality that
capture the diversity and divergence of our rural spaces. That means that we
must, to some degree, resist the urge to resort to our standard narratives.

OVERCOMING THE RURAL CHAPLAINCY

Rural small-membership congregations are deeply relational places. As Carl
Dudley points out, small congregations tend to operate as single-celled organ-
isms. Where large churches might have a variety of places for people to plug
in—small groups, committees, mission teams, and choirs—small churches
tend to have one main cell, which encompasses the majority, or even all, of the
congregation. Whereas each cell in a large church might have a slightly different focus, the single-celled church is primarily focused on congregational care.[1]

In these churches, relationships dictate how that care is distributed. New
members, for instance, may not instantly be welcomed into the community
of the church, and it might even take decades to be fully included in informal decision-making. Established members, meanwhile, will deliver food
to another established grieving family, both because they are both members
of the church, and because their histories and relationships are deeply intertwined. They are friends inside and outside of the church, and the relationships between families transcend firm boundaries. In the relational church,
categories like church, family, and friends have porous borders.

In small-membership churches, this means that relationships can become
the primary indicator of success for both the ministry of the church and the
success of the pastor. As Dudley notes, there are generally three types of
pastoral leadership: specialist, generalist, and lover. The specialists are usually found in churches with multiple staff members—there is a dedicated
person for pastoral care, for youth ministry, or outreach. In other churches,
the pastor must be a generalist, capable of handling all aspects of pastoral
ministry, including strategy, programs, and pastoral care. But, as Dudley tells
us, small-membership churches generally do not measure success through
effective programs. Rather, they measure their relationship with the pastor
first, followed by their general skills.[2]

In my first staff-parish relations committee meeting, I came armed with all
sorts of reports. I outlined my discipleship goals for the coming year, and how
those aligned with the various changes I was making to youth ministry and
Bible studies, as well as my upcoming sermon topics. I wanted to show that I
had clear goals for my first year, which was rooted in a substantial period of
listening sessions and feedback.

When we gathered, the committee glanced at my one-page synopsis, and
then set it aside. "Well, it seems to be going well. People like your preaching,

and people like you. They like that you show up. They feel like they're getting to know you, and that everyone has a good relationship with you." Twenty minutes later, the meeting had ended. My evaluation in that first session, as far as I could tell, stemmed from whether or not I was liked. For the most part, it seemed to have been finalized over meals and card games well before the meeting ever happened. The primary question, asked among friends and family: "What do you think of the new preacher?"

At the time, I was a part-time pastor, while I finished out a commitment at a university think-tank. There, my performance was measured primarily against the metrics of the grant that I managed. If I met the metrics of my grant and contributed to the general congeniality of the workplace, then I was successful. If not, then I would need to provide justification as to why I was unsuccessful. Personal relationships were important, but to a lesser extent.

It was both strange and daunting that so much depended on my likeability. Strange because for the majority of my life, I had been measured by what I produced: in school, it was grades. Professionally, it was my ability to manage a project. How can I know if I'm successful if the sole metric is whether I am liked? After all, very rarely does one come to you and say, "I do not like you."

Given that vagueness, being successful felt like a daunting challenge. What if my personality doesn't mesh well with someone? What if I make someone mad? What if their politics and my politics do not align? What if they think I'm weird? What if I think they're weird? What if I work hard and good things are happening, but at the end of the day, the staff-parish relations team chalks it up to, "But our personalities simply do not mesh?"

Depending on relationships without any sort of other standard of accountability can lead to several things going wrong. Obviously, leaders can be well-liked, good, and nice people, but their leadership can be entirely ineffective. Defaulting to the relationship can lead to organizational structures that are more designed to be without conflict than to further a mission. In moments where tension is necessary to produce growth and change, leaders can default to preserving amicability, and stymying potential.[3] Leaders can also, of course, cultivate cults of personality, absolving themselves from the work of forming a sustainable culture that moves forward in a cohesive vision.

This default to relationships also tends to perpetuate the myth of the agrarian paradise in unhelpful ways, wherein the only value of the rural church is the relationships it fosters. In his book, *The Gifts of The Small Church*, Jason Byassee interprets his own ministry in a rural church by using Wendell Berry's writings as his lens. In story after story, Byassee focuses on the relationships that are at work in the church, ultimately finding that the real value of the rural church is that it taught him what a church should be—humble, communal, curious, and committed—reflecting the stereotypes described in narratives about rural values.[4]

The danger here is obvious. If rural churches are pristine places where we find the best of Christianity, and the idyllic practices of Christian community lived out, then why should there be any change? Why should we engage deeply with the rural church? Rather than view them as places of vibrant ministry, these congregations become object lessons for future anecdotes about how great the church is. This limits the imagination about what the rural church can be for both members of the rural church and for the leaders, limiting the only possible course of ministry to be good, friendly, and loving people.

Rather than become a beacon of hope within the community, the idea of a purely relational church, or the idea that the pastor's sole job is to love the people within the congregation, can in fact be rather patronizing. It devalues the stories of the people in the church and leads us to think that the churches are not capable of any real or transformative work. It assumes that the people in rural congregations are not curious about their faith, or seeking to think critically about their lives in relation to the world around them. It imagines that people in rural congregations simply have no desire to "do ministry," a stereotype that is often imbued by rural pastors, even before they arrive at the congregation. Such a narrative becomes a way for pastors to shift the blame for a lack of ministry to the people of the church: my people just want me to love them, they expect and want nothing more. And, never having the opportunity or expectation to do or be more, the congregation lives into this self-fulfilling prophecy.

The default is starkly presented by Carl Dudley, who asserts that pastors who feel the need for consistent measurement "should not expect to find his or her calling satisfied" by rural, small-membership congregations. Pastors who can find their "reward with relationships," though, are well suited to these churches:

> As for a sense of achievement: on a Sunday morning, when the elderly parishioner who has slept through worship thanks the pastor for the sermon, the pastor of the caring cell will respond appropriately, "I love you, too."[5]

Is the reality that stark and bifurcated?

Simply put, no. In my own parish, I realized over time that my ability to connect with my parishioners was but one facet—even if it was a large one—of my performance. It mattered if people trusted me and felt comfortable sharing their concerns with me. At the same time, my parishioners wanted to see that we were growing in our faith together, and some of our best moments were when we hit the relief valve of pent up frustration, where we were able to talk openly about our future without fear of damaging our relationships. My parishioners, I realized, were curious people, who wanted to think deeply about the ways that God was calling them to live out their faith.

Key to this, though, was that we had a shared vision for our future. In our first six months, we spent time talking about where we felt the congregation was being called, and how that was different than where we stood now. When people quipped that they did not want to see the church change, I knew them well enough to know that they were really worried about losing certain components of the church. Creating a common vision took time, but it gave us a shared language. In turn, my evaluations became deeper—rather than see how well-liked I was, we paid attention to how much people were learning about scripture, opportunities for service, and whether they felt that I could be trusted with their pastoral care. There is no getting around the importance of relationships in a rural and small-membership church. But they need not limit the possibilities of the congregation.

In reflecting upon his own ministry, Jason Byassee writes that as he left his parish, he wondered if he had spent too much time in those relationships. He laments that his deepest achievement was to construct a new parsonage for the future pastor, an achievement that he fully recognizes is more for the clergy than for parishioners. If he could do it differently, he would have spent more time in the community, which in turn would help his parishioners understand the importance of reaching out beyond the walls of the church.[6]

As I headed into my first appointment, the most common advice I received was simple: love your parishioners. To be clear, that advice very much needs to be heeded. But, it cannot be heeded in such a way that commodifies our congregations to prove a theological point about the efficacy of community or the importance of relationships. Neither should that be advice that limits the potential for a ministerial or missional imagination. Rural churches can—and most definitely should—be places of vital, community ministry.

RESISTING DECLINE

There is no shortage of advice on how to make a church more vital. A quick glance at the bulk of literature, trainings, podcasts, and blogs on church leadership all point to the same general goal: making our churches grow.

The emphasis on church growth is not surprising. Over the last few decades, Christian denominations in the United States have been in a steady decline, losing church members and their attendance, volunteers, and funding. As a result, our churches and denominations, which tend to reflect contemporary business models, are forced to certain necessary realizations: either the business model must necessarily change due to a change in resources—both financial and otherwise—or we need to reverse the tide of decline.

For the most part, church leadership resources seek to do the latter through prescriptive remedies, while maintaining much of the same infrastructure. The hope is that by offering a series of best practices that can be acquired by the members of the organization—by churches, their pastors, and lay leaders—churches can reverse their decline.

The challenge, of course, is that most prescriptive methods are born out of a different time period, in a largely different culture. As Gil Rendle points out, the majority of church leadership techniques, and indeed our modern ideals of congregational life itself, are the fruits of a convergent culture. In a convergent culture, uniformity is prized, and it becomes the foundation for leadership. In the 1950s and 1960s, it was a cultural expectation that people attended church on a Sunday morning. Approaching and maintaining a level of uniformity was a desirable goal. And, as Rendle bluntly puts it, "It isn't difficult to lead people in the direction they are already going."[7]

In a divergent culture, however, difference is emphasized. These differences become the root of leadership.[8] In our culture, people value independence and their individuality. Shared experiences are fewer and more significant. Consider the numerous new expressions of faith that routinely pop up: theology on tap, coffeehouse small groups, dinner church. These are all designed to emphasize difference from conventionality, prioritizing divergence over convergence. The appeal is that they offer a unique experience from the "typical church."

In college, I decided that I no longer wanted to be affiliated with the denomination in which I had grown up. I realized I was not theologically aligned with many of their convictions, and so while I was not yet sure where I would find myself, I believed that it would be better to not be on the church's roll.

I communicated this to my mother, who cautioned against it. "It looks bad to not be a member of a church. Find a church you want to be a member of first."

The conversation showcases the difference between convergent and divergent cultures. My mother, a baby-boomer raised in a convergent community and time period, understood why I wanted to remove myself from my church's roll, but recognized a cultural significance to it. For her, it was expected that people be a member of a church, even if they did not necessarily identify with it. On the other hand, as someone who is solidly a millennial, I valued my theological identity more than cultural expectations. If my theology was significantly divergent from the institution, why would I remain? After all, no one ever asked to see proof of church membership, or even if I was a member of a church at all.

Assigned prescriptive practices are normally convergent. In order to flourish in the organization of a church or denomination, one must become attuned to convergent practices. Consider the way we select clergy. To be ordained in my own denomination, candidates are required to submit a number of assignments, including written theological reflections and videos of sermons.

The good intention of this is obvious. Before we ordain new pastors, we should evaluate their theology to ensure that it aligns with the broader church, and evaluate leadership practices, like sermons, to ensure fruitfulness.

Some of this can be done objectively. My denomination has certain theological standards that every pastor is expected to understand and teach. If someone cannot articulate a Wesleyan understanding of grace, then they will not be ordained to ministry, where teaching basic doctrines is expected.

The majority of these evaluations veer into subjective prescriptions, though, demanding convergence where it might not be necessary. Take preaching evaluations, for instance. Leonora Tubbs Tisdale argues that preaching is a form of local theology and folk art, part of the oral tradition in our communities. Preaching, most everyone agrees, should be contextual. Making a sermon contextual, as Tisdale tells us, is "fraught with risky choices."[9] Deciding whether a sermon should begin with an anecdote or scripture analysis, whether it should be concerned with global or local issues, how much emphasis should be given to application or theological teaching, and even how best to proclaim the sermon, are all contextual choices that a preacher must contend with on a regular basis.[10]

The evaluation of a sermon's effectiveness, likewise, must be contextual as well. Is the message of the sermon clear? If the preacher used an anecdote that does not make sense outside of the community, it might be clear to the members of the community, but not to an evaluator watching from hundreds of miles away. Was it stylistically well done? It depends. If a sermon is local folk art that beauty might not translate well to other settings and contexts. Was it preached well? If you prefer someone to preach without notes, you might find yourself bored by the preacher who is stationary behind the pulpit. If you enjoy the poetry of a written sermon, full of wordplay and beautiful prose, you might find yourself distracted by a preacher who paces across the floor with seemingly no thought to the shape and rhythm of their words.

All of these are highly subjective, evaluating without context the decisions weighed by the preacher for their local setting. By judging the sermons outside of that context, the denominational standards can easily revert to general prescriptions that are inherently convergent: we prefer you to preach without notes, for a sermon between fourteen to seventeen minutes, in a sermon series format.

The outcome, intended or not, enforces some level of uniformity. Those evaluating often do so with only their experiences of what is useful or not, and so they naturally want to see their own practices of success replicated.

The context of the evaluator can easily override the context of the candidate. To become a member of the organization requires no small degree of forced convergence, as candidates reshape themselves, temporarily or permanently, to meet the professional standards of those who have gone before them.

In this instance, imposing a standard of convergence is equated to a level of professionalism and success. While the church and the world might be increasingly divergent, professional standards demand a level of convergence. To deviate from those standards is to risk respect from peers and a loss of status within the organization. While accountability is never a bad thing, we should be careful about how we form our expectations and convergent standards, lest we impose standards that are maladapted to the context.

If the standard image of a successful congregation is a growing suburban or urban parish, then denominations and church leaders will naturally attempt to replicate that, without paying attention to the local divergences. Rural congregations, naturally, become the counterexample of this success. Not dissimilar from the larger public policy conversations, church growth experts will offer suggestions that assume that healthiness looks like suburbia.

Rural, small-membership churches may find that some of these prescriptions are useful, while others alienate them from the communities in which they are located. Regardless, rural congregations can often become trapped, accountable to a social narrative that is not theirs, with prescriptions that can do more harm than good.

The natural reaction to an unhelpful prescription is to reject it. A few years ago, I had a bad case of strep-throat. When I went to the doctor, I was given a shot of antibiotics. A few minutes later, my face had swollen up. Unbeknownst to me, I was allergic to the prescribed medicine. After some Benadryl, the doctor prescribed another antibiotic, and I went home.

Once home, I learned that I had a milder allergy to the second antibiotic. My options, as I saw them, were to either not take the medicine at all, and risk the strep-throat getting worse, or take the antibiotic and Benadryl at the same time, which would cause me to sleep much of the day away. I distrusted the doctor, who had now prescribed me two faulty medicines, and for a moment, I found myself wanting to dismiss their diagnosis outright.

When it comes to conversations about vitality and accountability, many rural congregations are in the same place. The side effects of the treatment have been as dangerous as the illness, and the diagnosis and expert opinion have been questionable. They feel trapped between wanting to get better and a treatment that doesn't work. So, they reject any conversation about vitality or accountability outright.

Fortunately for me, our small college has a clinic, run by a nurse-practitioner on faculty. When I relayed what had happened to her, she redid the strep-test to confirm the diagnosis, gave me new medication that helped, explained all of the side effects in detail, and followed up a few days later.

While I have argued that many of the standards of vitality are unhelpful prescriptions, I do not want to do outright reject the idea that rural congregations can and should have accountability so that they can become vital faith communities. Rather, I want offer a second opinion, of sorts. In order to do that, I want to explore how we arrive at our current standards of vitality, and then explore ways by which we might offer a new diagnosis and a new treatment plan, one that considers the divergence of rural communities.

THE CONTEXT OF VITALITY

How do we arrive at our standards of accountability? Accountability in mainline denominations is largely upward. The local church files report to the management above them, who sends it upward to the next level of management. In upward accountability, those at the top of the chain dictate the measurements that are requested. In the church, the primary metric is usually average worship attendance.

Measurements formed by the higher echelons of an organization are almost always convergent. Those at higher levels in an organization need to be able to quickly see how the organization is behaving. If a certain segment of the organization is behaving out of the norm, then the organization can go deeper and examine exactly why that is happening.[11]

A nationwide department store will look at sales for the previous quarter. If one region has slower sales, they will look at various contributors in that region. After they make an adjustment, sales once again become the standardized metric.

Top-down, convergent metrics also tend to be highly prescriptive, allowing the larger organization to make changes quickly. A nationwide department store might retrain the sales team, look at the products for sale in that region, or rethink the advertising. The goal is to find a solution that, through a series of changes, can fix the problem at hand. These prescriptive practices will not significantly change the business model, but rather ensure that the business model is able to run more effectively.

Churches are not dissimilar. In 2010, The United Methodist Church released the *Towers-Watson Report*, which describes traits of congregational vitality and how best to achieve it. Their results show that vital congregations have in common a series of indicators, grouped into four general areas:

1. Vital congregations provide multiple small groups, with more small groups and more programs for youth and children;

2. High percentage of effective lay leadership;
3. Worship services with a mix of traditional and contemporary services, alongside topical preaching;
4. Pastors who hold longer tenures and who excel at generative leadership.[12]

Importantly, this data is meant to be evaluative of the entirety of the denomination in North America. The report claims that churches in rural, urban, and suburban areas all had congregations that met standards of high vitality, and so these indicators became the template to which a vital congregation should be aspiring.

As a result, denominational officers at every level reinforce these goals. Continuing education events are assumed to be for everyone, because everyone needs to inhabit the same best practices, regardless of whether they are rural, suburban, or urban, and certainly regardless of size. This universality apparently proves the effectiveness of reports like *Towers-Watson*. When we dig deeper, though, we find that the universality of such metrics breaks down.

In order to conduct this particular evaluation, the steering committee listed metrics of a vital church. They then surveyed churches and denominational leaders to determine which churches were meeting those metrics. After looking at the list of churches that met those metrics, they compiled the results into indicators, or best practices, that would point toward vitality.

According to their results, large churches with an average worship attendance of 350 or more comprised the largest segment of the vital churches, at 41 percent. Medium-sized churches (100–349) accounted for another 29 percent.[13] While rural churches can be large, the majority of large churches tend to be located in urban and suburban areas. We know, too, that small-membership congregations are found in both suburban and urban environments, as well as rural spaces. So, according to *Towers-Watson*, only a small fraction of vital churches are located in rural places.

It is possible that it is harder for rural churches to be vital. More likely, though, is that the metrics chosen to represent vitality are more naturally suited to large churches in urban and suburban areas. Such a reality coincides with the prevailing rural narratives that we uncovered in chapter 1, wherein the standards of success are shaped by urban and suburban social memories.

A closer look at the indicators supports this. The authors report that "regardless of size, more vital churches have more programs for children (under 12 years old)."[14] This aligns with a truism of church leadership: the way we make our churches grow or become more vital is to make them younger.

In the first chapter, I briefly described Clay County, North Carolina. The county is nestled in the mountains of North Carolina, not too far from the Georgia and Tennessee state lines. Over the past few decades, its economy has shifted toward recreation. The town sits beside a lake, surrounded by mountains. People camp and play on the river, swim and ski in the lake, and hike in the mountains.

Because of its more temperate climate, the community has become an attractive place for retirees to settle. According to the U.S. Census Bureau, the small county grew mostly from domestic migration, with just over 3 percent of their growth coming from natural births. The over-65 population grew by almost 6 percent, while the under-eighteen population shrunk.

The county is home to several strong churches, including a mid-sized downtown church that sits adjacent to the town square. The church has seen steady growth, a large missional presence, and intentional faith development. They have committed and dedicate lay members, and strong pastoral leadership.

As part of a denomination effort to strengthen churches, a team of regional leaders met with church members to determine ways to continue strengthening the church. In these conversations, parishioners fondly remembered a large youth group from several years ago. The regional denominational leaders assigned to help strengthen the church more seized upon these desires, and in accordance with conventional wisdom, recommended in their report that the church focus on attracting and retaining teenagers and young adults.

It is a truism, and emphasized in our denomination's reports on vitality, that young churches indicate vitality. Yet, it is also a reality that the single fastest growing population in this community is recent retirees. For the surrounding community, these retirees are a benefit. They buy houses, contribute to the tax base, support (and even start) small businesses, and serve as volunteers and leaders in the community. They have, generally, larger amounts of disposable income and more time to offer. They have a wealth of experience from their careers that could be useful for any organization.

The conventional wisdom is that a community thrives when young adults abound, even as today's young adults have less disposable income, earn less than previous generations, and typically have less time to spend volunteering. The logic of young adults and young families being key to vitality is born out of the suburban experience, which primarily draws on young families. But, it is not true that young families are necessary for a vital and thriving community *or* a vital and thriving church.

At best, such advice encourages congregations to focus their attention and resources on populations that might be nonexistent in their communities. At worst, the advice ignores the blossoming and growing populations of people that need and want to find a way to live into community.

Another key indicator of vitality in *Towers-Watson* was a higher number of small groups, in general. Yet, in both small and very small congregations, the difference in the average number of groups between high vitality congregations and low vitality congregations was less than one, a statistically insignificant difference.[15] A small-membership church that functions as a single cell would be better off with one high impact small group than by trying to sustain a multitude of small groups.[16]

Reports like *Towers-Watson* have spawned a cottage industry of books for small churches that are seeking to grow. While it may be true that some small-membership churches are "not-yet-big-churches" in exurban or suburban areas, it is frequently not the case in rural communities where the population will not sustain rapid numeric growth.[17]

RURAL DIVERGENCE

Most of these resources assume that by adopting a few growth tactics that are tested and verified in urban and suburban settings, any church can add new members. Rural leaders who try technique after technique without the population to sustain such practices will quickly burn themselves out and frustrate their congregations.

In reality, the church as a whole is confronted with the issue of adapting to a divergent world. Increasingly, we engage with institutions in a variety of new ways. When my wife and I got married, we moved our checking account to her bank, and kept our savings account in mine. Because her bank has mobile deposits, and because most of our transactions are cashless, I have almost never stepped foot into a bank branch. Yet, I am still a member of that institution. I draw interest on my accounts that are housed there, and the checks that I write to my daughter's preschool bear their logo.

My wife, Abby, and I co-lead the youth group at our church. When we inherited the program, there were few high schoolers involved in Sunday School or the Sunday night youth activities. Meanwhile, a mentoring group had emerged, led by a few lay members of the congregation. The mentoring group paired girls in the community with a strong woman leader, and was combined with regular Bible studies.

By any standard of metric, the program is a success—it has fostered lay leadership in the church, a surprisingly large number of teenage girls attend, and data routinely shows that community mentors are foundational for success in life. Abby volunteers with the program, occasionally leading the Bible studies, and serving as a mentor. The question she most often gets, though, is unsurprising, if not disappointing: How do we get those girls to join in worship services or our regular youth meetings?

At one church council meeting, Abby encouraged church leaders to stop asking that question. Instead, she argued, we need to think about that group as an extension of the church. In reality, the majority of them will not come to Sunday School or youth group, which is comprised of mostly middle-schoolers. But, they are participating in the life of the church, and they are being formed as disciples. In fact, she highlighted, their participation is indicative of the church's success rather than a lack of vitality.

The fallacy in our current indicators of vitality is that they assume numeric growth is always possible and replicable, increasingly demanding standards not achievable in every location. Compounding that difficulty is the expectation that numerical growth will only happen in one of few areas: participation on Sunday morning or in a youth group meeting.

Rural communities, as we have seen, are incredibly complex places. They occupy roads that are seldom driven in isolated counties and the squares of bustling county seats. They are bound together quite literally only by the designation of "rural." The ideal of vitality must be measured differently in these places, reflecting the divergence of both rural places and the culture at large.

Here, I think rural churches—and the church as a whole—can learn something important from higher education. My wife and I both work at a small, private college. We rely on tuition and private donors to stay open, so that we might fulfill our mission of supporting our rural region.

If our primary metric was student enrollment (as a stand-in for average worship attendance), we could increase the number of students rapidly by offering free tuition, accepting every student even if they did not meet the minimum requirements of the program they choose. I am confident that we would grow, and quickly. Then, we would close.

This, of course, is why the number of students who show up on the first day of class is one metric among many. In order to be healthy and effective, we pay attention to a number of metrics, some set internally, and some set externally.

In addition to enrollment rates, we look at the amount of institutional aid given away, what percentage of students graduate, and how long it takes them to so. We pay attention to the general atmosphere on campus: Do students enjoy being here? Do faculty and staff enjoy working here? How many students return after their first semester? After their freshman year?

Some metrics are set by external bodies, and demand compliance. For instance, if more than 15 percent of nursing students fail their certification and licensing exams for too many semesters in a row, our nursing program will be placed on probation. These standards must be met.

But the majority of metrics have no guaranteed right answer. Instead, it's a balancing act between sustainability and achieving our mission, and a balancing act between metrics that emphasize uniformity, such as federal requirements for financial aid and accreditation standards, versus divergent metrics, those things that we pay attention to that helps us fulfill our unique mission. This means that a healthy college can be small or large, urban or rural, highly selective or have open enrollment. In some cases, we can actually enroll fewer students and actually be healthier college. Each college must have a clear vision and pay close attention to the metrics that support and move them toward that vision.

My college, for instance, is a rural, denominationally affiliated school. Because of that, we work hard to ensure access to rural students and to United Methodist students by offering substantial tuition discounts. We make sure that, alongside our indicators of effectiveness and financial health, we are paying attention to ensuring access once students arrive on campus, and how first-generation college students are able to navigate things like course registration and financial aid forms. We know that we will not be competing with Vanderbilt, whose campus is an hour away. That helps us stay focused on what makes us thrive in our mission.

Likewise, rural congregations may not be able to become large churches, and that's ok. My college will never be a large one. That does not mean we cannot be effective, missional, and healthy.

RESETTING ACCOUNTABILITY

So far, I have argued that our perceptions of the rural congregations and church vitality closely mirror the narratives of rural communities as a whole. On the one hand, rural churches are seen as deeply relational places, where meaningful and transformational ministry is limited by the churches need to simply be loved and perpetuate a caring cell. At the same time, our standard indicators of vitality are born out of a convergent model of success found in suburban and urban contexts.

Neither of these is sufficient to cultivate vital ministry in a rural congregation. Because rural communities are complex and divergent, they require indicators that foster vitality at the local level, respecting both the deeply relational aspects and the necessity of fostering and living out a shared vision.

Deciding indicators of vitality at the local level is a fairly significant shift in accountability for most churches. As I've highlighted, standards of accountability are often set by denominational leaders, and such indicators are predominantly convergent. They are also often what we call lagging indicators, meaning that they can only measure what has happened in the past, which cannot be changed. There is no way to know if average worship attendance will go up or down until after it's happened, at which point it is too late to change it.

Some churches might feel pressure to have downward accountability, as well. If a church has a food pantry or a daycare, there will be accountability to the clients who use those services. Again, these are usually lagging indicators:

Did we provide enough food this month, or did we close for weather so many days that parents are upset?

For the local church, these are all external levels of accountability. They report out what is happening to people not in the organization. External accountability emphasizes obligations. When those obligations are not met, the organization anticipates some amount consequences.[18] If average worship attendance does not increase, the pastor's regional leaders may request the pastor take a continuing education class, or even look at closing the church. If clients of the food pantry do not receive food, the ministry may have to close. If parents feel the daycare is closed too many days out of the year, they may withdraw their tuition dollars.

What many churches struggle with is to develop internal measures of accountability which focus on a shared responsibility.[19] For pastors, this is exceptionally difficult, as pastors have both upward accountability to their denominational managers, and downward accountability to the parishioners who evaluate them, control their salaries, and can influence their mental and emotional health and well-being.[20]

Determining how best to measure vitality is a conversation that should start, first and foremost, among the congregation. That means that congregations should be developing internal measurements of success that point toward a clear goal, and not rely solely on the metrics assigned to them by stakeholders above or below them on the denominational organizational chart. These internal metrics of vitality will no doubt be divergent, exemplifying the best of the local church, accounting for the weaknesses of the congregation, and driving toward a vision of meaningful and transformative ministry.

THE UNIQUE ASSETS OF THE RURAL CHURCH

Rather than default to standard narratives or assumptions, organizations need to pay attention to their immediate assets. Rural churches often have several strengths that are relatively unique to their own social and geographic location, and that might not immediately translate to larger churches or churches in urban and suburban settings.

First, rural churches are permanent stakeholders in their communities. Often, the local church is one of the oldest, if not the oldest, of institutions in the community. Hospitals struggle to stay open, newspapers fold, small businesses come and go, and even schools might close or merge. Many of our rural churches, though, have displayed a remarkable resiliency, as the same few families congregate week after week for a century of more. These churches have a long social memory, and have witnessed the whole of the community.

Second, rural churches are still trusted institutions in rural communities. Rural communities tend to be more religious, and the local church is still seen as a trustworthy institution. While people might be skeptical and even embarrassed to seek mental healthcare at a county clinic, for instance, they display little shame meeting the pastor for coffee, or heading into the fellowship hall for a meeting. Because they are ingrained into the DNA of the community, the rural church carries a level of trust that other organizations, particularly outside organizations, do not.

Third, rural churches are one of only a few places where a cross-section of the community shows up each week. A few years ago, I was at an event with a colleague who worked in public policy. In the room, we had gathered a wide variety of community leaders: health care professionals, business owners, teachers, and local elected officials.

My colleague leaned over to me and whispered, "I wish there was a way to get a group like this together more frequently."

"There is," I replied. "They show up at my church every week."

In our church's pews, I had retired college professors, teachers, nurses, an occupational therapy graduate student, and small-business owners. Aside from places like Rotary Club, we were the only place where this cross-sector group gathered on a weekly basis. And, unlike Rotary, people gathered in our sanctuary each representing their whole self, and not simply their profession.

When these unique assets are combined, we notice that rural congregations have a unique—and frankly enviable—position in the community. They are places that can speak to the story and life of the community, they are respected and trusted, and they have the potential for multiple perspectives and strengths from across the community. When rural churches understand these strengths, they can recognize and act upon their position as community leaders and agents of community change.

INDICATORS OF A THRIVING
RURAL CONGREGATION

In the coming chapters, I will argue that a vital rural congregation is one that recognizes and acts on its ability to lead the wider community to participate in the Kingdom of God. This is, I believe, a theological, social, and evangelical vision for the rural church. There are a myriad of ways to live out that vision, but cultivating and living out this vision requires organizational practices that draw from and support our theology and goals. Otherwise, they are all but doomed to fail.

For the remainder of this chapter, I want to explore three indicators that can help congregations sustain such a vision. Two caveats are important. First, these indicators are not metrics in themselves. Rather, they are indicators that encourage congregations to move accountability away from only the typical up-/downflow, and instead reclaim the ability to set internal standards that chart their progress, based on the context they are in. Some of these measurements will be quantitative, counting raw numbers and interpreting that. Some will be qualitative, encouraging stories that highlight growth and progress toward goals.

Second, you will likely notice several common indicators not mentioned here. You will not find any conversation about average worship attendance or a growing youth group, for example. These things might be important to other aspects of your church—sustainability or community empowerment, for instance—but they might not be the primary driver of every vital congregation.

Indicator One: A Thriving Rural Church Has a Clear Theological Identity

Every organization needs a clear focus and mission, around which the practices of the organization are built. For congregations, our theology is that foundation. In theory, that seems obvious; in practice, it is usually a bit more difficult.

When I lead workshops, I like to do a quick activity. First, I have the group shout out what makes a church a church: What are those essential qualities that a church just has to have? The answers are never very surprising. A church has to have a worship service, committees, and a budget. They are places of community; they have a building, and some programs. They have Sunday School, and they obviously need Jesus and the Holy Spirit.

After we make a long list, I ask the group a slightly different question: If they could only select three items from that list to start a church with, which three items would they pick? The participants write their answers on sticky notes and pass them up, where we tally the responses.

More often than not, the answers reveal a bias toward organizational structure. If they could only carry over three things, the church leaders tend to want to carry over the things they spend the most amount of time worrying about, like money, volunteers, and good programs.

This is not too surprising. Spirituality is often seen as deeply personal. Theology is viewed as theoretical, often without any real implication to operations. The church should support those things, but there is often no clear vision as to how the church should go about that work. The primary goal, then, becomes staying open and operational. So, goals turn to the practical: How do we get more money? How can we recruit more volunteers?

Then, depending on the resources available, we can turn our attention to focusing on the idealistic goals, those more ethereal things like theology and spirituality.

Organizational structure does matter, but in many scenarios, it can dictate the theological vision of the church rather than empower and support the vision. This is not dissimilar from other organizations, even businesses, whose strategies can become complicated, vast and unmanageable. Lack of a clear focus leads, inevitably, to mission creep, wherein the mission is amended and added onto over time, so that in the end, the original mission either exists in name only or not at all.

For the church, theology is not just about mission and productivity. Our beliefs should permeate the culture. Sermons are not just events that happen; they invite people to understand how Jesus might interact with their lives outside of the church walls. Bible studies equip parishioners to read the Bible well. People are curious to learn about and explore the mystery of God. This is a culture that must be cultivated.

Key to this is the recovery of vocation within the church. In contemporary parlance, the term *vocation* has a professional connotation. Within the church, it is often understood to be about a vocation to a particular task within the Christian organization—a call to ordained ministry or a role as a lay-staff person. Because the conversation about vocation has generally been connected to work and career, our discussions become limited to work in institutionalized ministry.

The theologically grounded church cultivates a sense of vocation for each member, wherein they can articulate the ways that Christ is calling them to live out their faith in the world around them. For some, that might be ordained ministry or service in the congregation. For others, that might be helping them to understand their secular careers in light of their faith.

A young adult in my previous congregation had a natural talent for working with kids and youth, and so I invited her to be one of the youth leaders. She was exceptionally gifted at the work. She easily connected with the students, intuitively knowing how to connect across age groups and social statuses. In truth, she would make an excellent ordained pastor, and so I tried to get her to consider that vocation by offering increasing responsibility within the youth group. After about a year, I invited her to begin leading the youth group, hoping that she would take over, while I played a supporting role.

She declined. At first, she cited her busy schedule. She was pursuing her master's degree in occupational therapy, and she would be away during the week, even if she would be back in time for our Sunday night gathering. She also shared that she did not feel comfortable leading youth lessons; she was not trained to teach the Bible, and she did not want that particular responsibility.

In our conversations, I slowly recognized that she was not called to ordained ministry, and that it was not my place to try to persuade her to pursue ordination. Though she would be an exceptional clergy person, she had no clear calling to that work. She could, though, clearly articulate a call to be an occupational therapist. She talked about a God who created each individual with differing abilities. Her way of living out her faith, her vocation, was to be a resource to those who are differently abled. She was especially passionate about kids, particularly kids on the autism spectrum. When her vocation interacts with the church, it will be through her future work as an occupational therapist.

In trying to persuade her to attend seminary and be ordained, I eventually came to recognize an important distinction for my own role in helping my parishioners discover their vocation. Rather than naming gifts and offering preset pathways, like committee work or ordained ministry, I needed to begin helping them think through how they might take their next most faithful step with their God-given gifts. For this young adult, the most faithful step would not be ordination, and potentially a future career that only uses a few of her talents and skills. Rather, it was to live out her sense of vocation, grounded in a clear theological identity.

A church with a clear theological identity can produce laity who connect their lives to a sense of Divine call, uncovering what it means for them to be faithful as a business owner, a teacher, an elected official, or a scientist. A vital church is a place to form people who can, with a deep and grounded theology, respond to God's call, with "This is what I have been equipped to do."

Indicator 2: A Thriving Rural Church Has a Commitment to Community

As I noted earlier, rural churches are often one of only a few permanent stakeholders in a community. Hospitals are closing at alarming rates, businesses come and go, and even schools merge and close over time. Churches, though, have long a presence in the community. They have seen how the community has changed and grown over the years.

A vital congregation takes that a step further, connecting the story of the community to the story of God. They can see how God has been and is at work in the community, and they are eager to join in with that work. These churches can understand and discuss the joys and pains of the community, and how they have contributed to both. They eagerly look to uncover potential and opportunities, and they see themselves among the assets of a community.

As churches seek to uncover the story of their community, they must be careful not to default to preexisting narratives. Small-membership churches naturally tend to default to the caring cell, which can narrow the story

significantly. A church of middle-class senior citizens might believe that
the entire community looks and acts like they do: aging, retired, and with a
strong social circle. Without talking to any other members of the community,
they have unwittingly defaulted to a narrow narrative about their place, leaving out young adults, working professionals, other income levels, and other
demographics.

Increasingly, churches make use of demographic data to help broaden the
perspective of the community. Programs like *MissionInsite* or even Census
reports can uncover some interesting realities about the communities. Data,
though, is only ever one side of the story.

Each summer, my parish had a summer feeding ministry. To help us think
through how we might expand that ministry, our congregation applied for
and received a summer fellow, sponsored by a nearby foundation. The fellow was a college senior, studying public policy. Her first task was to do a
broad asset map of the area. We limited the radius to a fifteen-minute drive
from the church, and she began mapping out the various organizations that
we might partner with, as well as opportunities for us to engage in the community around us.

On her first day, we did a short drive tour through the area, which was
rapidly growing with retirees from the nearby metropolitan areas. When our
fellow pulled the average income of our neighbors, she noted that they were
rather wealthy. Still, she noted that this seemed incongruous with her experience in the community.

The data was accurate: we were located in a generally wealthy area. The
narrative was different. We could point to pockets of poverty, including the
roughly fifty families who showed up twice a month for food. When we put
the narrative and the data together, we realized that our best work would be
to serve those pockets of poverty. In a blog post for the sponsoring foundation, our fellow pointed out that while large foundations would be reluctant
to pour resources into an area like ours, there were still pockets of poverty
sandwiched between high-income areas. The church, she noted, was uniquely
positioned to fill that gap.[21] Relying fully on the data would not have helped
us come to that conclusion, or plan our work, as we would not have seen a
need to do feeding ministries in a high-wealth area. Meanwhile, relying on
the narrative would have made us too broad and less effective. We would not
have been able to target our resources appropriately.

The balance between narrative and data is a necessary one. Each year, my
center offers a small Community Transformation Grant for United Methodist
congregations in rural Tennessee. In the first iteration, we awarded the grant
to a group of nineteen churches to lead a summer literacy program. The
leaders of the project had a holistic view of the community. They knew the
strengths of the volunteers, many of who were retired educators. They knew

the literacy rates of their community, and could talk about the national statistics that emphasize the importance of reading at grade level by the third grade. They knew the challenges of the members of the community.

At every stage, the leaders of the program could connect the dots between data and narrative to uncover the full story. Each morning, one of the pastors rode the bus to pick up and drop off the participants, and she could tell you the reason why each child struggled to read. They even spent time selecting which church would be the site of the daily activities, making sure that the church was central enough to the participant's houses, but still close enough to downtown and school to be familiar.

A congregation committed to the community knows that community well. And, because of their theological and spiritual formation, they know their responsibility to the community. They are taking steps to live out that responsibility in creative and imaginative ways, utilizing the resources they find along the way.

Indicator Three: A Thriving Rural Church Practices Good Stewardship

Generally, when churches talk about stewardship, they tend to immediately focus on financial stewardship. Within rural, small-membership churches, these conversations are anxious ones. A member of the finance committee might stand before the church as the fiscal year draws to a close, reminding members to increase their giving to make ends meet. In December, letters and announcements remind me to give more.

As a pastor, I typically dreaded our budget writing process. We struggled to project how tithes and offerings might change, struggled to see where we could reduce overhead costs, prioritized which maintenance projects we try to get done, and how much we needed to raise in fundraisers. Generally, our programming budget was any of the anticipated income not used for operations. The budget, in all honesty, was less of a strategic document, and more a plan for survival: this is how we will use the resources you give us to stay afloat through these next twelve months.

In many of our small-membership churches, this is the full conversation about stewardship: How do we raise the necessary funds to continue existing in our current form, so that we might remain open?

For the thriving rural congregation, though, this should be the most basic level of stewardship. A thriving rural congregation should obviously be able to cover the cost of overhead, keeping the lights on and the doors open. Such a narrow view of stewardship, though, will unfortunately narrow missional imaginations, forfeiting the opportunity to explore the full assets of the congregation.

In truth, churches generally work with far more assets than they realize. Volunteers provide countless in-kind hours, members regularly donate
materials, saving the church money. Church property that goes unused
throughout the week means that billions of dollars' worth of assets are
being underutilized, while every community has groups looking for meeting
spaces.

The congregation I attend has a small, two-story house, on the property
that is designated for the youth to use on Sundays. During the week, though,
a nonprofit that works with child abuse victims uses the house. Cameras have
been installed upstairs in the most comfortable seating areas, so that coun-
selors can conduct interviews which are monitored in other rooms by court-
appointed officials, in order to prevent the trauma of having a child appear as
a witness in court. On Sundays, our youth have Sunday School and Sunday
night gatherings.

It may not be possible to launch a multitude of ministries within the congregation; after all, most rural church budgets cannot sustain ongoing programs
in trauma counseling for childhood abuse victims, which requires highly
specialized professionals and specific equipment. By opening the space to the
community, though, the church is ensuring that this vital ministry takes place.
Using the building in this way also ensures that church is interconnected with
the wider community. Simply put, this is good stewardship of resources that
would otherwise go unused.

Ultimately, practicing good stewardship means that churches are making
use of all the resources at their disposal. Recognizing and deploying these
resources requires a great deal of creativity, a creativity that will be increasingly necessary in the next few decades. Millennials, the oldest of whom are
now in their late-thirties, have lower levels of disposable income, higher debt
ratios, and less retirement savings. Generation Z will follow many of those
same trends, while amplifying the gig-economy, driven by short-term con-
tracts rather than long-term salaried positions. These generations will have
less disposable income as they move into the position of supporting local
congregations.

As churches practice good stewardship, they will need to consider both
mission and structure. To be blunt, the rural church's greatest missional
resource is not usually their finances. Churches will not be leaders in the community simply based on the amount of money they pour into mission projects.
Rather, churches should be clear about the assets they bring to the table, and
what role they might play in the existing community ecosystem. What are
the strengths and talents of the people in the congregation? What other community groups and organizations are doing work in the areas in which your
church is interested? Are they effective? If so, how might your church partner
to fill their needs? Can your space be an asset? Do you have volunteers?

Churches will also need to pay attention to their organizational structure. For some churches, this might mean rotating leaders through existing committees. For others, this may mean redefining the number and the roles of the various committees. Still for other churches, this may require a close look at staffing needs: Does the church need a full-time pastor, or would a bivocational pastor be a bigger asset? Does a church have enough staff? Or might volunteers fill some of the roles? Small-membership congregations have an innate ability to be nimble.[22]

Good stewardship means that churches are utilizing all of their resources to live out their vocation as a congregation. Grounded in their theological identity and commitment to community, they can name their assets, cultivate partnerships, and deploy their resources to help the wider community recognize the reality of the Kingdom of God.

MEANINGFUL MINISTRY

I remember telling my new seminary classmates that after graduation, I would serve in a rural church, a stipulation of my scholarship. There were surprised glances and sympathetic eyes. Basic math dictates that because these churches tend to make up the overwhelming majority of congregations, most pastors will serve in a rural parish, if only for a brief time. Still, the standard of success was to be named as an associate pastor at a larger church.

Since then, I try to pay attention to the way rural pastors, myself included, describe their ministry. Often, they are apologetic. Once, at a dinner for rural pastors, each clergy person stood up to describe their ministries with the same basic script. "I serve two churches, the largest one has 25," or, "We don't have many kids, and we only average around 60 in worship."

With imaginations beset by the "grow or die" mindset, they wanted to know how to attract more people to worship, even as their community's population stagnated. Or, they sought to launch youth programs in the midst of new retiree communities. These pastors had come to believe that the best metrics were ones that we were ill-suited for their contexts.

Toward the end of the evening, we changed the conversation, inviting pastors to share where they saw the Kingdom of God at work around them. Suddenly, the mood shifted. The group talked about feeding ministries that fed hundreds each month, and about after-school tutoring programs that were making a difference in the community. They talked about the ways that youth and children were leading in their church. Why, I wondered, did we not start with those stories?

As I have argued throughout this chapter, I think we presume those deficiencies because these churches have tried to adhere to a notion of viability that was not engineered for their communities and contexts. These churches need better indicators for what it means to thrive.

Let me conclude this chapter by stating an obvious fact: not every rural church will survive. Likewise, not every urban and suburban church will survive. But the death of the rural church is also not a guarantee.

The rural church has a unique opportunity to be agents of transformation in their communities. In order to do so, the rural church needs to claim a vision of vitality that understandings their own theological identity, practices a sincere commitment to the community, and practice sustainable leadership in new and creative ways. By doing so, these churches will open themselves up to a path of evangelism that recognizes, cultivates, announces, and invites the wider community to participate in Kingdom of God.

NOTES

1. Dudley, Carl S. *Effective Small Churches in the Twenty-First Century.* Nashville: Abingdon Press, 2003. 37–50.

2. Ibid., 80–81.

3. Rendle, Gilbert R. *Quietly Courageous: Leading the Church in a Changing World.* Rowman & Littlefield, 2019. 97.

4. Byassee, Jason. *The Gifts of the Small Church.* Nashville, TN: Abingdon Press, 2010. 97, 107, 109.

5. Dudley, *Effective Small Churches in the Twenty-first Century*, 83.

6. Ibid., 96.

7. Rendle, *Quietly Courageous*, 36.

8. Ibid., 35.

9. Tisdale, Leonora Tubbs. *Preaching as Local Theology and Folk Art.* Fortress Press, 2010. 93.

10. Ibid.

11. Ebrahim, Alnoor. *The Many Faces of Nonprofit Accountability.* Harvard Business School, 2010. 1–32. Here I cite a working paper from the author, which is a preprint of a chapter in The Jossey-Bass Handbook of Nonprofit Leadership and Management (Third Edition, 2010).

12. De Wetter, David, Ilene Gochman, Rich Luss, and Rick Sherwood. "UMC Call to Action: Vital Congregations Research Project." Report. Nashville, TN: United Methodist Church, 2010. 46–126; 3.

13. Ibid., 24.

14. Ibid., 31.

15. Ibid., 30.

16. Dudley, *Effective Small Churches in the Twenty-first Century*, 37.

17. I borrow the term "not-yet-big-churches" from the book Kotan, Kay, and Phil Schroeder. *Small Church Checkup: Assessing Your Church's Health and Creating a Treatment Plan.* Abingdon, 2018.

18. Ebrahim, *The Many Faces of Nonprofit Accountability*, 3.

19. Ibid.

20. Rendle, *Quietly Courageous*, 127.

21. Lee, Alison. "She Sparks: Fellow Alison Lee Reflects on Her Time with JKHF and Merritt's Chapel United Methodist Church." *Medium*, August 22, 2017, medium.com/@jamiekirkhahn/she-sparks-fellow-alison-lee-reflects-on-her-time-with-jkhf-and-merritts-chapel-united-methodist-fd2010bd6e6a.

22. Fischbeck, Lisa G. "Lisa G. Fischbeck: The Strength and Beauty of Small Churches." *Faith and Leadership*, July 15, 2013, faithandleadership.com/lisa-g-fischbeck-strength-and-beauty-small-churches.

Chapter 3

Reclaiming Evangelism

The indicators presented in chapter 2 are meant to guide rural congregations in rethinking and reclaiming their own narrative of vitality. More importantly, churches who align with these indicators reveal themselves to be well suited for leadership both within and outside of the walls of the church. These congregations are able to ground themselves in a clear mission, rooted in their theology; they understand their communities; and they are more adept at understanding all of the resources of their particular community ecosystem, including their partners for ministry.

A natural output of this vitality is that the rural church is positioned to be a leader within the community. They find that, with their unique assets, the expertise and gifts within their congregation and community, and their position as permanent stakeholders, they are often the one of a few organizations within the community that can lead meaningful and transformational work.

The challenge these vital congregations face is how to understand this work in such a way that it complements their theological identity, rather than disconnecting their faith so that they retain only the essence of a good nonprofit. This is not to fault the work of nonprofits, of course, but rather to lay claim to an essential truth about the nature of the church: the church exists first and foremost because of its theological identity, namely a commitment to the lordship of Jesus Christ. Because of this reality, the work that flows out of the church should always have a distinctive marker, a pearl formed over the 2,000 years of our faith, that points to a different reality. The vocation of the church is different than the vocation of the nonprofit, even if they both achieve some of the same goals along the way.

In some cases, the church has been uneasy about this reality. Some churches view missions and outreach as a means of bolstering attendance on a Sunday morning. The view is that as churches connect to the wider community, the community will begin to recognize that the church is a place of good, join into that work, and begin to attend. This is not necessarily wrong, and in fact might be true. There is no guarantee, though, that a strong missional presence will increase average worship attendance, nor should that be the primary motivation of the church in mission. When Jesus fed the 5,000 in the Gospel of Matthew, the motivation was not singularly rooted in a desire to attract followers.[1]

On the other end, some churches view missions and outreach as entirely distinctive from the worshipping life of the community. In these congregations, the priority of local missions is simply to be a social witness. As an overcorrection to trying to view missions as a recruitment, some congregations will completely distance themselves from all but the shallowest of theological reflection. A congregation might launch into a feeding ministry based on the ideal that God does not desire people to go hungry, which is true. Still, Jesus feeding the crowds was not just about feeding the hungry. It was first and foremost a moment when Jesus revealed an image of the Kingdom of God. It forced the disciples and the crowd to witness a miracle of generosity, while affirming an essential truth of the Kingdom of God, an echo of the Exodus story: in God's reign, there is always enough. Here, we are reminded of God's manna in the wilderness as Jesus produces plenty from essentially nothing. It was a stark reminder of how God intends for the Kingdom of God to function.

A church focused on community development, or any mission, purely for the sake of "doing good" will be avoiding an essential theological component of the mission of the church. Alternatively, a church with the sole motivation of using missions as a way to increase average worship attendance will be sorely misdirected.

For rural congregations in particular, these two justifications—church growth or social witness—might actually be seen as a justification *not* to be in serious mission. In a rural community that has seen significant population decline, a rural church that sees little hope of growing in average worship attendance will see no benefit to doing missions as a way of promoting growth. Conversely, in rural communities where congregations are made up of people in disparate economic backgrounds, the focus on social good might be first and foremost promoting the welfare of the people in the congregation. Why expand into the surrounding community when there are existing needs within the church itself?

As I have argued, rural churches have a responsibility as a permanent stakeholder to be leaders of community transformation. Such work is a natural outpouring of the vital and thriving rural congregation. They do not have the luxury, simply put, of disengaging from the wider life of the community.

The question remains, though: How does the vital rural congregation frame this work? How should a church understand community leadership in a theologically responsible way, stemming from their theological identity, commitment to community, and stewardship of resources? And how do they avoid such work being separated and distinct from their identity of vitality?

To answer that, I believe that the vital rural church engages in a practice of community development as evangelism. More specifically, the practice of community development as evangelism is one that recognizes, cultivates, announces, and invites the wider community to participate in the Kingdom of God.

THE FRAMEWORK OF EVANGELISM

In many mainline congregations, the word "evangelism" will often be met with some confusion or resistance. Generally, evangelism is seen innocently enough, bearing the intention of inviting people to experience the grace of Jesus Christ and the love of God in a transformative way.[2] In theory, I take no real issue with such a definition, as it seems quite logical. Just as I invite people to experience restaurants that I enjoy, to read books and see movies that moved me, and to pull for sports teams that I am fond of, it makes sense that I would invite someone to experience a faith that has become the central identifying marker of my life—after all, it has shaped my career, the ethics I live by, and the way my wife and I understand our responsibility as parents and partners.

In practice, evangelism is understood in multiple ways. Within contemporary culture, it often corresponds closely with proclamation. Our most notable evangelist, for instance, is Billy Graham, whose main work was in preaching and writing, with an emphasis on conversion. Graham's evangelism, which did reflect a commitment to critical theology, gave way to televangelists who know of no such commitment.[3] At their worst, these televangelists can promote rather harmful theology, while encouraging viewers to make substantial donations that benefit none but the televangelist.[4]

Proclamation is not the only form of evangelism. The term *evangelize* is a term that literally means to offer "good news." As such, it is not a surprise that theologians such as John Wesley and Charles Grandison Finney understood evangelism to be proclamation in part, but also inviting social reform efforts and compassionate efforts, as well as small groups focused on discipleship formation.[5]

As Laceye Warner points out, proclamation began to supplant these other practices when William Tyndale used the term "preach" instead of "evangelize" in his biblical translation. This led to an overemphasis on the work of proclamation, and as Warner aptly states, "the richness of the language related to evangelism has been lost."[6]

Given our diminished view of evangelism, it is helpful to think about both what evangelism is not, and what it is intended to be. The goal, of course, is not to deconstruct for the sake of deconstructing, but rather to offer a foundation to point toward creative and life-giving opportunities for grounding the work of the local church as agents of transformation within the Kingdom of God.

WHAT EVANGELISM IS NOT

In trying to dictate what evangelism is, it's easier to begin by saying what evangelism is not. As we have already seen, the practice of evangelism is severely limited when it is confined to just the work of proclamation. Historically speaking, restricting the practice of evangelism to only proclamation excluded some Christians from practicing evangelism at all. If preaching was the ultimate act of evangelism, then women, who were not able to be ordained or licensed as preachers, were unable to serve as evangelists.[7]

Reducing the work of evangelism to proclamation also leaves out a critical component of the conversion experience: the formation of the disciple in a Christian community. As a high-schooler, I attended mission trips with my youth group. At the beginning of each week, the mission trip would begin with some training in evangelism, wherein we would practice giving our testimony, culminating in asking our conversation partner to invite Christ into their lives. If the person did convert, we were to instruct the person to find a church where they could become active disciples. Our work would be done, and the relationship would be over.

By reducing evangelism to this form of proclamation, we can inadvertently remove ourselves from the relational aspect of the Gospel and place the onus of faith formation on the person we are attempting to evangelize. While the Great Commission's imperative is to make disciples, such a shallow view of evangelism risks leaving that work to the would-be disciple, abdicating the evangelist's role in the most critical part of faith formation. As William Abraham argues, this can unfortunately result in "the isolation of evangelism from the full ministry of the church."[8]

If limiting evangelism to proclamation risks isolation from the full ministry of church, promoting evangelism as a tactic by which to increase average worship attendance faults in the other extreme. For many congregations, the work of evangelism is not about an invitation into the Kingdom of God, or the formation of disciples into the Kingdom of God, but rather it has shifted to focus on the recruitment of new members of the local congregation. Largely, I believe this comes from a confusion around the language itself, where "disciple" has become co-opted to mean "member," and so "evangelism" means "recruitment." At best, such an understanding is what Trevor Hart refers to as a "slippage of sign," wherein the language of our discourse is intrinsically and constantly unstable, rendering a meaningful conversation on practice unintelligible.[9] At worst, this is what Bryan Stone refers to as *evangelistic cheating*, focused on a particular end, in this case average worship attendance, and "disregard[s] or trivialize[s] the integrity of the practice itself."[10]

Evangelism is also not analogous to marketing and communications. While evangelism does require a commitment to communication—after all, it requires sharing the good news—a slick marketing campaign is not in and of itself the work of evangelism. To borrow from Stone again, this work is *trifling*, disinterested in the motivations of the practice of evangelism, and instead aims to be able to point to the busywork that these efforts have produced.[11]

Reducing evangelism to proclamation, recruitment, and marketing does carry the benefit of simplifying our efforts, but truncates its meaningfulness. Isolated proclamation removes the burden from the speaker to carry the listener forward into the formational process, placing the onus on the hearer, rather than the shared burden of Christian community. Recruitment lowers the standard of discipleship substantially, so that the measure of success is not a community that is, to borrow from John Wesley, spreading scriptural holiness, but rather a growth in attendance. The production of marketing materials as an evangelical practice removes even the basest of personal interaction, without which evangelism cannot survive.

WHAT EVANGELISM IS

Defining evangelism completely would be a daunting task. That task is for another book, and other theologians. In reality, the practices of evangelism are varied across the denominational and theological spectrum. To reiterate, it is easier to say what evangelism is not than it is to say precisely what it is. Rather than define evangelism in and of itself, I want to look at some characteristics of the wider practice of evangelism, and identify some guardrails that offer guidance to the practice of evangelism.

First is the motivation for the work of evangelism. If the goal is not to attract new members in the church, then what is it for? As William Abraham posits, evangelism is less about the recruitment of new members, and is instead more focused on the work of initiating people into the Kingdom of God.[12] For Abraham, this is a series of intentional activities that lead a person to learn and practice the grammar of the church. Through this, the person being evangelized (1) is linked to a community; (2) begins to understand the "intellectual and theological vision" of the church; (3) adheres to a basic standard of biblical morality; (4) receives an assurance from the Holy Spirit; (5) can identify their spiritual gifts; (6) begins to serve within the Kingdom of God; and (7) takes up spiritual disciplines, chief among them fasting, prayer, reading the scripture, and sharing in communion.[13]

This understanding of evangelism offers a much deeper understanding of the practice of evangelism than our typical notions of conversion. As Warner notes, there is often a desire to separate the practices of discipleship and discipleship formation as distinct from the work of evangelism. But, as Warner rightly argues, if it is true that evangelism is at the core of the church's mission—and it is hard to argue that it is not, given the clear directive of the Great Commission—then evangelism must also "be the core of our ecclesial practices."[14] This means that evangelism cannot easily be separated from the holistic life of the church, as they are intertwined together in purpose and form.

Likewise, Bryan Stone emphasizes this deep connection when he argues that "evangelism is not so much *a* practice as an intrinsic characteristic of *every* Christian practice and of the comprehensive praxis of Christian faith itself."[15] While I am wary to say that every practice of the church is a practice of evangelism in and of itself, Stone's argument that evangelism as a practice is a natural outgrowth of the Christian life is one that is well-received. To live into a Christian ethic, and to embody the practices of the church, is to live out a witness of our faith.

This brings us to the heart of the motivation for evangelism. While the practices of evangelism might entail the deeper work of discipleship formation, the underlying motivation that is at the heart of evangelism is help people live into the present realities of the Kingdom of God, and to be inaugurated as citizens into that kingdom.

It is necessary, I think, to state explicitly what I mean when I say that the ultimate goal is to inaugurate people into the Kingdom of God, or when I reference the present realities of that kingdom. Often, such language is over-spiritualized, so that the Kingdom of God becomes a distinctive, post-earthly reality. This hyper-spiritualization reasons that the Kingdom of God cannot be experienced until after we die, because the full vision of God will not be realized until the final days, when the full glory of Christ is revealed, as shown in Revelation 21:1-6, and in particular, verses 3-4:

See, the home of God is among mortals.
He will dwell with them;
they will be his peoples,
and God himself will be with them;
he will wipe every tear from their eyes.
Death will be no more;
mourning and crying and pain will be no more,
for the first things have passed away.

Of course, it would be silly to argue that this vision is fully realized in the present world. We can obviously see pain and death in our world. Clearly, the Kingdom of God is something to be anticipated. And yet, the disciples and the early church spoke about the Kingdom of God as if it were a present reality. Consider, for instance, the instructions that Jesus gives to the seventy in Luke 10. Whether the disciples were well-received or not, in whatever community they visited they were expected to share a similar message: "The Kingdom of God has come near to you."[16]

Likewise, after the resurrection and ascension of Christ, the disciples begin to form in communities that exemplified a Christian ethic of the Kingdom of Heaven. In Acts, there is a clear desire to live into a social and economic reality that is markedly different from that of the wider Roman culture, as the converts to Christianity make a habit of sharing their possessions rather than retaining personal property.[17]

In less drastic ways, the Kingdom of God is revealed through markedly counterculture experiences. Consider the narrative of Luke 10:38–42, where Jesus invites women to sit and learn, a strange social action in a deeply patriarchal society. Likewise, Jesus upended the idea of status when he voluntarily washed the feet of his disciples, a task typically reserved for the lowest in the social food chain.[18] And, perhaps most significantly, the trial of Jesus is centered around the claim that Jesus is King, a pointed threat to the existing emperor and political entities of the day.[19]

Clearly, there is some indication that the Kingdom of God is present, even if it is not yet fully revealed. In his groundbreaking book, *Announcing the Reign of God*, Mortimer Arias puts it like this:

> The kingdom of God *has come*; it is experience of good news centered in Jesus and his ministry. The kingdom of God *will come*; it is hope, tense expectation, the mobilizing promise projected towards its final consummation. At the same time, the kingdom *is coming*; in the midst of conflict, it is the center of a tremendous struggle of cosmic proportions that calls forth a confrontation.[20]

John Wesley, the founder of Methodism provides a helpful way of understanding this already-but-not-yet view of the Kingdom of God. Wesley tended to think of the Kingdom of God as having two dimensions. The first is the Kingdom of Glory, which is understood only when one experiences the fullness of God's presence, which will not be realized in this lifetime. The second, the Kingdom of Grace, is the dimension of God's eternal kingdom that is already present. To participate in the Kingdom of Grace is understood to be more than just simply acquiescing to a faith. Rather, participation in the Kingdom of Grace is both about personal practices of Christianity and about a clear social witness. In this Wesleyan theology, a personal faith and a social witness are inseparable, as our faith requires us to reorient our communities toward the Kingdom of Grace.[21] For Wesley and the early Methodists, this meant developing schools, establishing clear economic practices (e.g., a ban on high-interest loans), advocating for quality healthcare, and other practices.

This reality sets up a pivotal need within the church to embody a practice that is distinctive from the wider world, formed through a moral and ethical reality that is grounded in scripture. Obviously, such work takes a great deal of time and effort, which is why the work of evangelism must necessarily be committed to the formation of the disciple as they begin to live into this new reality.

Given this here-but-not-yet-present nature of the Kingdom of God, the task of evangelism is to help people begin to renarrate their own lives in light of that kingdom. This means that the church must be able to offer something distinctive to the wider community. In the same way that Jesus feeding the 5,000 revealed something about the nature of the Kingdom of God—particularly that of hospitality, gratitude, and the reality of God's provision—the church's actions must also reveal something of the nature of this kingdom, so that the wider community might catch a glimpse of what God is doing in this world, and how they can participate in this new reality of God's present kingdom.

In doing so, the church is able to help people renarrate their own stories, and their vocations and lives, so that they too can join in the work of the Kingdom of God. William Abraham writes that evangelism "arises out of the inauguration of God's sovereign rule on earth, and its central aim is to see people firmly grounded with that rule so that they can begin a new life as agents of reconciliation, compassion, and peace."[22] To be in mission in the church is to be part of the mission of God, or the *missio Dei*. The practices of evangelism are motivated in an effort to help people understand the realities of God's Kingdom, to orient people to life in the kingdom, and to begin their own vocation within the Kingdom of God.

Obviously, such work requires guard rails. Adapting from the lessons offered by Laceye Warner's profile of women evangelists and social reformers in the nineteenth and early twentieth centuries, we can identify at least five criteria for this work.[23] First, it is necessarily open to all; it cannot be limited to those with whom we are naturally inclined to join in community. Second, evangelism grapples with the realities of sin within ourselves and within our social realities. It is necessary to recognize that the present realities of our world are often antithetical to the ethics of the Kingdom of God, whether those be moral, economic, political, or social in nature. Third, there is a clear focus on conversion. While that language might be uncomfortable to some, I want to reiterate that the notion of conversion here is focused on initiating people into the citizenship in the Kingdom of God. As we will see later in this chapter, I do not believe that such work is meant to be coercive or pressure filled. Neither is it a short-term process, but rather it is rooted in longer relationships. Third, evangelism necessarily keeps a focus on sanctification. It follows then that the fourth criterion is to help the church understand and begin to join in the mission of the church, which is rooted in Christ's love of the world, and has a dedication to serve to the world. Lastly, such work must inherently be grounded in scripture. Without a vivid scriptural imagination, the work of evangelism might easily be skewed into something with alternative motives and different ends.

COMMUNITY DEVELOPMENT AS EVANGELISM

With the understanding about what evangelism is and is not, we can turn toward the notion of community development—or more broadly, community engagement—as a practice of evangelism for the vital rural church. Acknowledging that rural churches are not always positioned to attract new members or find unchurched people, I offer this understanding of community development as evangelism as a framework through which rural congregations can understand and practice their unique role as stakeholders in their communities, while helping the wider community experience the realities and presence of the Kingdom of God.

In the next chapter, I will look at some of the tensions in leading community development work, and how rooting such work in evangelism helps us to overcome those challenges. Chapter 5 will examine some case studies of churches who have done this work well. For the rest of this chapter, though, I want to explore the definition of evangelism as community development that I offered at the outset of the chapter: community development as evangelism is the work of recognizing, cultivating, announcing, and inviting the wider community to participate in the Kingdom of God.

Those who have done work in community or economic development will find that this framework naturally follows a practice of Asset Based Community Development. I have no real interest in rethinking the toolkit available to congregations because there are ample strategies to help congregations think through the nuts and bolts of such work. Instead, I want to help rural congregations make a clearer connection between their theological commitments and their practices, so that the two are inseparable. Reframing community development as a process for evangelism helps us to do that by ensuring that we are mindful that our work is connected to the salvific work of Jesus Christ for the redemption of the whole world.

Before exploring this framework for practicing evangelism, I want to make a brief aside about the work of community development. Typically, such work is seen as broad systematic work, but it need not be. Local communities and economies are complex, and in a small town, changing one or two variables can have a tremendous impact. Broadly speaking, community development can be any number of activities that improve life within the community, whether that is through directly improving the economic conditions or health of people, or by supporting initiatives that add cultural enrichment.[24] Churches should not be overwhelmed at the notion of doing community development, but rather be empowered to live into their ability to create meaningful change in the community—whether that is by teaching a child to read at grade level, or by reducing homelessness. In doing so, they will help their communities embrace the theological and social realities of God's very present kingdom.

RECOGNIZING THE KINGDOM OF GOD

My friend Meghan copastors a small-membership church with her husband. The congregation exemplifies the church embedded in the community, with a meaningful ministry to -the homeless, and a commitment to sharing in the work of social justice. Meghan often leads workshops on community engagement, and begins each one with a list of her own assumptions about church leadership. The most compelling, and one that usually brings about a moment of quiet reflection from the pastors in the room, is her assumption that God's prevenient grace is actually at work in the community. For her, it is a foundational component to the work that she does in community leadership, and her question to the pastors in the room is innocent, yet pointed: "Do we actually believe that God is at work in our communities? If not, why are we here?"

Prevenient grace is one of the hallmarks of John Wesleyan's theology, a theology that is grounded in a robust theology of grace. In his sermon "On Working Out Our Own Salvation," Wesley works through Philippians 2:12-13, emphasizing that God makes the first move in our salvation. This initial move from God is what we refer to as *prevenient grace*, which comes from an older interpretation of *preventing*, meaning "to go before." A simpler understanding is that this is the grace of God that is already present in us, and in the world around us. Wesley argues that "everyone has some measure of that light, some glimmering ray, which, sooner or later, more or less, enlightens every" person.[25]

As Wesley understands our path to salvation, it is only because of God's initial work that we are able to respond to what God is doing, and therefore, we are able to begin "working out our own faith."[26] Our faith, then, is a response to the grace and love of God which has already been poured out.

If we are to understand the work of community development as a means of initiating the wider community into the Kingdom of God, then the first task is to identify where we are able to locate the Kingdom of God. Just as we begin our faith journey by recognizing that God's grace is present long before we are able to discern it, we must begin by recognizing that God has been at work in our communities long before we are able to perceive it.

Finding these places where God is at work can be difficult, particularly in congregations that have long believed that they have little value and few assets. This is why it is important for the congregations and their leaders to be able to properly narrate the story of both their community and their congregation, as we discovered in chapter 1. Churches should be able to recognize the prevailing narratives that shape how they understand their contexts, and be ready and able to correct those narratives when needed.

If we believe that God is working to reveal God's Kingdom, then we also ought to believe that through God's grace, we have been equipped to engage in that work. After all, as we have seen, evangelism is a central component of the church's mission, and evangelism is meant to initiate people into the Kingdom of God.

Identifying all of the places where God is at work, though, can prove to be a daunting task, or quickly become idealized. It is true, for instance, to say that God is at work in all of creation all the time. But while this is no doubt true, it is of no practical value to make this obvious claim. A congregation, regardless of their size and resources, cannot engage with all of creation at any point in time.

The challenge becomes attempting to name specific instances of where God is at work around us. Thriving churches, as described in the previous chapter, will have made some progress toward this already, as they are able to name their own theological identity, and identify their own resources. The most natural place to begin this work, then, is within the life of the local church.

Here, we can borrow from the practices of Asset Based Community Development (ABCD), which is rooted in the premise that communities can lead substantive change by utilizing the often-unseen strengths that exist within the community already. Rather than outsource solutions to a governmental or outside group, ABCD seeks to build upon the existing social fabric of a community. The result is a stronger community fabric.[27]

As we look at the work of the congregation, we should pay close attention to the skills and experiences that people bring into the church setting. Typically, over the course of a career, members of congregations amass valuable skills and knowledge, which does not disappear when they walk through the doors of the sanctuary on Sunday morning. Likewise, people cultivate skills in their hobbies that can be particularly useful to work in the community. Though it has nothing to do with my professional life, I play the guitar and a few other instruments, and in turn, I teach those to middle-schoolers in our church. Someone else might be quite adept at woodworking, sewing, or any number of things.

We should also pay close attention to the other intangible and tangible assets. Intangible assets might present themselves through the values of the congregations. Rather than completely dispel traditions, congregations might recognize that traditions represent particular values that can be foundation for their work, serving as a compass in cultivating partnerships and planning.

Tangibly, congregations sometimes fail to recognize their most prominent asset—their property. It's a truism that civic groups in the United States are declining. Fewer people are participating in groups such as Rotary, Boy Scouts, and Kiwanis. At the same time though, as millennials find their way back to small towns and rural areas, they are not completely disengaging from life in the community.[28] People in this generation, who are now into their thirties and approaching forty, are more committed to volunteering than previous generations, even though they might not be engaged in civic organizations.[29] Instead, they are forming their own civic networks, launching nonprofits that support their volunteer efforts and hobbies.[30] These nonprofits are often small, and lack any real infrastructure. In rural areas, churches might easily become an accessible meeting space for these groups, ensuring both a connection between the new nonprofits and the church, and strengthening the bond between the church and the community.

Property can be a valuable asset in connecting to the community. My previous congregation had a large gym, which we seldom used during the week. One of our high-schoolers was a talented basketball player, who had received a scholarship to a small college nearby. His parents had purchased a used rebounding machine, a tall piece of equipment that is difficult to store. Because our gym had two basketball goals, he and his father approached us about storing the shooting machine in the church, and whether he would be able to practice there once a week. In exchange, they would supervise open shoot nights for other students in the area. By the time the student graduated, it was not uncommon to find his whole basketball team practicing in our gym, running drills under his father's guidance.

While our congregations hold a great number of assets, we should be certain to look out into the wider community as well. If we believe in prevenient grace, then we should believe that God's work is not limited to the confines of the local church. One obvious place to start is to begin by mapping out the nonprofits in the area, and discovering what work is already being done.

Doing the work of identifying where God has already begun to work in the community is important, because of a few reasons. First, it prevents the congregation from believing that the God's grace is limited to the work of the community. Second, it enables the church to see the wider ecosystem, gaining an appreciation for the work of partners of which they otherwise might not have been aware. Third, it enables congregations to be better stewards of their resources, offering their own assets to a partnership without needlessly replicating someone else's efforts.

A few years ago, my congregation began thinking about new missional projects that we might do. In the midst of this conversation, one of the members of the congregation was approached by a neighboring nonprofit that focused on providing food to low-income families during the summer. They needed a distribution center near the elementary school, and volunteers to help give out the food. Every other week, they would bring enough food for the fifty-odd families that would come through, and we would sort it and distribute it.

It was a remarkably simple program that cost us very little. And it was a ministry that, on our own, we would not have been able to do. The logistics were overseen by the nonprofit agency; the costs were paid for through a large grant. We just provided volunteers and space. By recognizing that other nonprofits were at work in the community, we were able to join in a meaningful program in our community.

CULTIVATING THE KINGDOM OF GOD

Recognizing the Kingdom of God demands that we pay attention to the work that God is doing in our communities and congregations ahead of us. In that sense, it is essentially the work of recognizing where God's prevenient grace is already at work.

Continuing in that same template, the work of cultivating the Kingdom of God might be best understood through Wesley's articulation of justifying grace. In Wesleyan theology, God's grace warrants a response. To be justified in God follows an acceptance of an invitation from God, through grace. As Albert Outler and Randy Maddox both emphasize, the pardoning that is offered in God's grace is also an empowerment. That is, we are pardoned so that we can be empowered to follow God.[31]

In the same way, we are not called to recognize the work of the Kingdom of God so that we can simply observe. Instead, the ability to see the tremendous assets of our congregations and communities empowers us to begin the work of cultivating the Kingdom of God in thoughtful ways. We are called to be responsible partners in God's work in the world.

The work of cultivation can be slow and often meandering. In the fundraising world, we often speak of cultivating donors. This cultivation often takes months or even years, as the fundraiser works to understand the motivations and passions of the donor, so that, when the time comes, the donor feels a sense of ownership over the work to be done with the gift, believes in the project, and trusts the institution to which they gave. Such work almost never travels a straight line. Rather, it is formed through meals, coffees, office and home visits, and phone conversations.

Similarly, cultivating the Kingdom of God can be a slow process as well. Congregations should begin this work with the assets, strengths, and resources they uncovered as they began to recognize where God is at work. As they look over these resources, they should look for natural connections. They might notice, for instance, that a literacy program needs volunteer teachers, and many of the parishioners are retired educators. These natural connections provide a space to immediately plug in to the work already happening.

In some communities, identifying nonprofits will be a relatively short exercise—the church, a school, the county government, and a volunteer fire department may very well be the totality of potential partnerships. Here, churches might consider acting as a convener, drawing together representatives from all of these places to talk about the needs of the community, and what small actionable items might be accomplished to address those needs, utilizing the resources that each agency brings to the table.

In the work of cultivation, congregations should bear in mind two important realities. First, churches should remind themselves that God has been and continues to be at work throughout the community. Rather than assume that churches will naturally be leading the initial work of cultivation, they should be mindful that they will often be joining in as junior partners. In many communities, churches might be the last organization to join in the conversation. Rather than presume leadership, churches should seek to embody the servant-hood template of Christ.

Second, congregations should be mindful that the work of cultivation is not the end of the work. In fundraising, donors will often give an initial small gift. This is rarely the last gift that they will make; if that relationship is stewarded well, they will likely make more significant or recurring contributions in the future. In the same way, beginning to volunteer with an existing nonprofit should be seen as an initial step in a relationship, like a first coffee between two friends. Volunteering in another nonprofit's activities should not be seen as the end goal, but rather an initial step toward something bigger.

In truth, this relieves some of the pressure of leading wide scale, community transformation. By concentrating on immediate and changeable variables, congregations can make forward progress, building goodwill in the community, and the capacity to launch more transformative work over time.

Wesley's understanding of justification echoes this reality. While Christians are at times tempted to end their spiritual journey of salvation at justification, Wesley emphasized that justification was an empowerment for moving closer to God.[32] Rather than seeing cultivation as the end product, the intentionally small steps taken in the work of cultivation should be rendered as the initial work toward a bigger imagination, an initial stretching of our muscles before we begin to exercise.

ANNOUNCING THE KINGDOM OF GOD

In Wesley's theology, sanctification was a lengthy process, and the bulk of the Christian journey. To live into sanctifying grace was to be drawn into a habit of growth. This emphasis on "growth in grace" pointed to the dualistic outputs of our Christian life—one, we grow in spiritually, and two, in so doing we become closer to God, growth that helps us to live out an ethic reminiscent of that which Christ commands. All of this is a result of God's working in us, and our own response to that work.[33] Ultimately, a life of sanctification leads to what Wesley refers to as "Christian Perfection," an often misunderstood term.

In John Wesley's theology, Christian Perfection was less about a state of flawlessness, in which people make absolutely no mistakes. Indeed, Wesley recognized that a perfectly sinless life was all but impossible. Rather, Christian Perfection might be best understood as a reliance upon God's grace, wherein the practices of faith become less of a struggle, and more natural. As people depend upon the love and grace of God, they are more equipped to reflect that love and grace to the wider world.[34]

Ultimately, the sanctifying grace that Wesley emphasized was understood as an inward spiritual change that led to an outwardly changed life. When we consider how our community development announces the Kingdom of God, we should consider it a reflection of this same "growth in grace"; a growth that begins with an inward transformation, but ultimately reveals itself through the lived realities of our church in the community.

As the church begins to respond to the gifts, pains, and hopes of the wider community, their ability to announce the Kingdom of God begins internally. Namely, congregations understand their work to be connected to their own spiritual growth, as well as an output of their spiritual maturity

At the outset of this chapter, I highlighted a very real tension in the motivation of congregations who are engaged in meaningful community work. Often, the work of missions becomes disconnected from the theological foundation of the congregation. What we refer to as "local missions," or more pertinent to our conversation, as community engagement and development, has always played a pivotal role in spiritual formation within Wesleyan theology.

Wesley articulated a variety of practices, which he refers to as "means of grace." These he defines as "outward signs, words, or actions, ordained of God, and appointed for this end, to be ordinary channels whereby [God] might convey to [humanity] preventing [or prevenient], justifying, or sanctifying grace."[35] In short, the means of grace are those actions which communicate God's grace to us as we perform them. Obviously, these include actions such as communion, prayer, and scripture, though they are not limited to these.

When it comes to sanctifying grace, Wesley urged what he referred to as "works of mercy." This wide-ranging category encompassed much of our typical social ministries—including education, feeding ministries, healthcare, and others—demonstrating a clear and natural "connection between love of God and love of others."[36]

Our ability to announce the Kingdom of God, then, begins first in the ability to recognize that our community engagement is in fact an act of spiritual obedience, and that through that work, God is drawing us closer to God's-self. In doing so, we must practice naming explicitly the habits of our faith that we are living out, beyond simply doing good deeds.

When congregations begin to engage with neighbors with whom they typically do not engage, for instance, the church might articulate that they are practicing a type of confession, confessing that there are people in the community they have not seen or known. As they place themselves in a service role, serving as a "junior partner" with other organizations, they might name that they are in an act of repentance, demonstrating a desire to form new relationships.

To practice announcing the reign of God is not to proselytize, or walk through the streets wearing sandwich-board signs that urge people to repent. Rather, it is the ability to name that the work being done is meant to reveal something about who Jesus is, both to ourselves and to the wider community.

The pinnacle of this ability to announce the Kingdom of God, then, is to be able to fully answer the question, "Why are you doing this?" with a sincere "Because through grace, God has called and equipped me to this work, and because I believe this is what the Kingdom of God looks like. I want the whole of my community to experience that grace, too."

INVITING THE COMMUNITY TO PARTICIPATE IN GOD'S KINGDOM

When I began teaching a bible study on evangelism, the first question that I got was, "When do we have to invite people to church?" Understandably, there was a certain amount of trepidation. Some of my parishioners were wary about offending someone or being imposing. For others, they legitimately might not have known anyone who lacked a church.

In practicing an evangelism of community engagement and development, the ultimate goal is not intended to be an invitation into the life of the local church, though that might be a natural output. Rather, the goal is to invite members of the community to understand what we ourselves discover as we grow in our faith—that the Kingdom of God has implications for the way we structure our communities; that God cares about more than just the spiritual dimensions, but also the economic and social realities of our communities. To live out the social realities requires us to take up certain practices, those means of grace, so that we can become attuned to God's transformational grace.

As we do this work, we in turn invite the members of our communities to begin to habituate themselves into those same practices. As we practice our own confession, we invite others to internalize this practice as well. As we embody community, we serve as an example of Christian community.

In many settings, these practices are already performed, even if they are not named as such. A few years ago, I was invited to help coordinate a regional gathering of rural and urban leaders. Our goal was to emphasize that with the region, we needed to understand the connectedness and interdependence between the rural and urban areas. At each table was a variety of leaders from the various towns—business owners, elected officials, teachers, and clergy.

As the night began, the participants were encouraged to lay out their assumptions about the other geography—rural leaders shared their perspective of urban communities, and urban leaders shared their perspectives of rural places. In the midst of our conversation, the participants all communicated a mistrust and faulty assumptions of the other communities. The rural leaders at my table, whose primary economic experience with urban communities was through local manufacturers owned by urban companies, thought deeply about urban blight and the high poverty rates in some of the urban communities. Meanwhile, the urban leaders recognized that almost none of the plant managers lived in the rural communities, meaning that the rural places who supplied the plant's low-wage labor did not reap the benefits of the highest income remaining in their communities.

As we uncovered these surprises, the leaders began to talk about how they might adjust business practices, expand access to social care programs, and emphasize the clear connectedness between the rural and urban communities. The conversations continued over dinner for the next hour.

Within this example, you can see clear habits of the church, though they are not articulated as such. The participants at my table practiced a form of confession, as they recognized their own failure to understand the other communities. Then, they moved to a beginning of repentance, exploring how to prevent future harm. Lastly, we engaged in a communal meal, a less sacramental form of communion. While they did not know it, they began to practice the habits of the church, the practices of spiritual and ecclesial formation.

The church's job in doing the work of community development as we discover, is not, first and foremost, about the economic ends. Rather, it is about helping the community experience the Kingdom of God by recognizing a counter social narrative to that of our conventional politics. It is about doing good, yes, but it is really an attempt by the church to join with those sent out by Jesus in Luke 10, saying with humility, "The Kingdom of God has come near to you."

The result of that kingdom? Transformed social relationships, mentors who invest in a young person's life, a renewed sense of vocation for entering into the postretirement chapter of their life, liberation for the poor and oppressed, and opportunities for people to live well. Such practices echo the words of Mary's song in Luke 1, when she sings that the birth of Jesus will reform the social and economic structure of the world, bringing the world into alignment with "promise made to our ancestors, to Abraham and his descendants forever."[37]

Conceptualizing community development as evangelism is a way of helping the wider community remember a distinctive story about who they are. Remembering this story is not just informational, whereby we convince people to join our congregations or appeal to a logical or even emotional argument. Rather it is remembered through the distinctive practices of the church, as the community recognizes that the church is an instrument of hospitality, unhesitant to lead confession and begin the work of repentance, and to invite people to sit at the table of Christ.

As the church itself understands its work as a means of grace, the wider community becomes saturated and habituated into the same rhythm of responding to grace. They themselves are able to recognize the gifts of the community, join in that work, and respond to it in meaningful ways. The work begun in the church points the wider community to the beginning and end of our faith—the one who comes for the transformation and redemption of the world.

The counterargument to this approach, of course, is that it does not necessarily have a defining moment of conversion. There is no singular moment when a member of the local congregation demands that the wider community acquiesce to the demands of the Christian faith. While there is an emphasis on conversion, it is a conversion of habituation, rather than a conversion found in a single moment.

This is meant to offer a deeper way to engage in the story of God's reign. As Bryan Stone argues, "Christians become Christians not merely by hearing a story, but by being formed bodily into one. Only as this happens can we become faithful tellers and enactors of that story in the world that is watching and listening, even when we are tempted to think it is not."[38] As we ourselves become faithful practitioners of this story, as we become participants in what God is doing in the community, we in turn tell that story to a wider community. Through this, we invite them into a transformation of their own. In doing so, we anticipate that God's grace is indeed at work, that they become initiated into the same practices of recognition, cultivation, announcement, and invitation, until ultimately they too are participants in revealing the realities of the Kingdom of God.

TRANSFORMING EVANGELISM

One of the leading failures of the rural church, as I hope I have made clear, is not that they are places that lack vitality. Neither is it that they are places that invite no growth. Rather, the failure is that these churches have not always seized the opportunity to practice any transformational leadership in their community, despite the positions of influence they hold in these places. The ability of a rural church to offer hope to their community, to correct the narrative of decline or plateau is a failure to join in the redeeming work of what God is doing. To again invoke William Abraham, our work in the wider community should be a means by which people "encounter a transcendent reality that has entered history to find oneself drawn up into the ultimate purposes of God for history and creation."[39] In rural communities, the ability to lead this transformation is not just a side project of a vital church, it is the work of a vital church that is offering hope to a wider community.

It is also deeply biblical. Consider the story of Zacchaeus in Luke 19:1–10. Jesus is passing through a community, and Zacchaeus desperately wants to see him. As a tax collector who had stolen a great deal from the community, and as a short man, he could neither see Jesus passing, nor was the crowd predisposed to help him see. So Zacchaeus climbs a tree. Jesus sees him in the tree limbs and *recognizes* that Zacchaeus has a sense of longing and a desire for community. Jesus *cultivates* this, inviting himself over to lunch. This welcoming into community is an *announcement* of God's Kingdom. It scandalizes the crowd, who are seeing a new sort of community form, an alternative reality to their dislike of this man. Zacchaeus, understanding this to be the community of God, repents and gives away half of his possessions plus a quadruple repayment of anything he stole—not a small economic impact. Jesus *invites* Zacchaeus to participate in this Kingdom of God by renarrating Zacchaeus's life, reminding him that "he too is a son of Abraham." In doing so, Jesus not only invited Zacchaeus to the work of economic impact, but to renarrate his life in light of God's transformational work in our world.

The vital rural church, likewise, is called to remind the community who they are in light of the Kingdom of God. That starts within the congregation itself, as they live into the prevenient grace extended to us, learning to recognize the ways that God is already at work. The church responds to what God is doing by cultivating, or partnering, in that grace, embodying what it means to respond responsibly to God's justifying grace. Congregations must do the hard work of naming their own sanctification, learning to identify the means of grace, and how they practice them, as they begin to announce the reality of God's Kingdom. And, as the church seizes its responsibility to be a leader in the community, they in turn invite the wider community to participate in that work, to engage in the habits of God's Kingdom.

The rural church, to reemphasize, is a place with unique assets: they are trusted, they are generally one of the few permanent institutions, and they have a unique connection to the community through the people who gather weekly. The vitality of these institutions, ultimately, is not just about the health of the congregation. Rather, their vitality is deeply connected to the community itself. Their evangelism, likewise, is not about attracting new members, but a necessary and foundational practice that ought to reside at the heart of the rural church. As key stakeholders, the rural church must embrace its natural role as community leader. By understanding evangelism and community development as two facets of the same work, rural churches better equip themselves to be agents of reconciliation, hope, and transformation as they help the wider community recognize the new life that the Kingdom of God brings.

NOTES

1. Mathew 14:13-21.

2. See, for instance, Knight, Henry H., and F. Douglas Powe. *Transforming Evangelism: The Wesleyan Way of Sharing Faith*. Discipleship Resources, 2013, who define evangelism as "sharing and inviting others to experience the good new that God loves and invites us into a transforming relationship through which we are forgiven, receive new life, and are restored to the image of God."

3. Abraham, William J. *The Logic of Evangelism*. Eerdmans, 2006. 9–19.

4. Brice-Saddler, Michael. "A Wealthy Televangelist Explains His Fleet of Private Jets: 'It's a Biblical Thing'." *The Washington Post, WP Company*, June 4, 2019, www.washingtonpost.com/religion/2019/06/04/wealthy-televangelist-explains -his-fleet-private-jets-its-biblical-thing/.

5. Warner, Laceye C. *Saving Women: Retrieving Evangelistic Theology and Practice*. Waco: Baylor University Press, 2007. 8.

6. Ibid., 9.

7. Ibid., 8.

8. Abraham, *The Logic of Evangelism*, 69.

9. Hart, Trevor. *Between the Image and the Word*. Routledge, 2013. 114.

10. Stone, Bryan P. *Evangelism after Christendom: The Theology and Practice of Christian Witness*. Brazos Press, 2007. 33.

11. Ibid.

12. Abraham, *The Logic of Evangelism*, 95.

13. Ibid., 102–3.

14. Warner, *Saving Women*, 278.

15. Stone, *Evangelism after Christendom*, 27.

16. Luke 10:9–11.

17. Acts 2:44–45, Acts 5:32–37.

18. John 13:1–17.

19. Luke 23.

20. Arias, Mortimer. *Announcing the Reign of God: Evangelization and the Subversive Memory of Jesus*. Fortress Press, 1984. 42.

21. Maddox, Randy L. *Responsible Grace: John Wesley's Practical Theology*. Kingswood Books, 1994. 244.

22. Abraham, *The Logic of Evangelism*, 101.

23. Warner, *Saving Women*, 280. Here, I borrow from Warner's 5 understandings and practices.

24. Theodori, Gene L. "Community and Community Development in Resource-Based Areas: Operational Definitions Rooted in an Interactional Perspective." *Society & Natural Resources* 18, no. 7 (2005): 661–69. doi:10.1080/08941920590959640.

25. Wesley, John. Sermon 85, III.4, "On Working Out Our Own Salvation," http://wesley.nnu.edu/john-wesley/the-sermons-of-john-wesley-1872-edition/sermon-85-on-working-out-our-own-salvation/.

26. Ibid., III.3.

27. "ABCD Toolkit: What Is Asset Based Community Development?" Collaborative for Neighborhood Transformation, https://resources.depaul.edu/abcd-institute/resources/Documents/WhatisAssetBasedCommunityDevelopment.pdf.

28. Brown, Jeffrey, and Mike Fritz. "Why Millennials Are Moving Away from Large Urban Centers." *PBS, Public Broadcasting Service*, December 2, 2019, www.pbs.org/newshour/show/why-millennials-are-moving-away-from-large-urban-centers.

29. "More Millennials Value Volunteering Than Previous Generation Did." *Philanthropy News Digest (PND)*, January 5, 2015, philanthropynewsdigest.org/news/more-millennials-value-volunteering-than-previous-generation-did.

30. Aamot, Gregg, and Gregg AamotGregg Aamot. "Nonprofits, Mirroring a National Trend, Grow in Minnesota's Smallest Places." *MinnPost*, August 28, 2015, www.minnpost.com/rural-dispatches/2015/08/nonprofits-mirroring-national-trend-grow-minnesota-s-smallest-places/.

31. Maddox, *Responsible Grace*, 168.

32. Ibid., 170.

33. Ibid., 177–79.

34. Ibid., 188.

35. Wesley, John. Sermon 16, II.1, "The Means of Grace," http://wesley.nnu.edu/john-wesley/the-sermons-of-john-wesley-1872-edition/sermon-16-the-means-of-grace/.

36. Maddox, *Responsible Grace*, 215.

37. Luke 1:46–55.

38. Stone, *Evangelism after Christendom*, 56.

39. Abraham, *The Logic of Evangelism*, 101.

Chapter 4

Reclaiming Our Theological Goals

Several years ago, I found myself in a church fellowship hall working with a group of pastors, volunteers, and community leaders to think about how the group might begin new efforts in community development. Over the course of several meetings, we had taken stock of our assets, looked closely at the needs within the community, and identified a diverse group of partners to ensure that the whole community was represented. There was a feeling in the room that the group was poised to begin leading something missional, new, and innovative.

The impasse came when we began to talk about exactly what the work should look like. For some, the most obvious first step was to build off the services that were providing basic needs, like the local food pantry. This met an obvious need, and if it expanded, it could feed more families in the county.

For others, meeting basic needs was a step in the wrong direction. It was better, they said, to offer "a hand-up instead of a handout." Others focused on the lack of relationship with the people that were being served. How were we able to be the church if we were not engaging in any sort of meaningful relationship? Others still focused on the lack of emphasis on justice, arguing that we were not doing enough to change the economic and community systems that had allowed for conditions that fostered a community where hunger existed. A few grew frustrated with what they felt was a theoretical conversation, eager to start working and figuring the rest out as they progressed.

These tensions are not new and quite common. Churches have taken a myriad of approaches to community development. Some congregations emphasize short-term work aimed at providing immediate aid or charity. Some might offer after-school tutoring to students in low-performing schools. Other congregations approach community development as a work of political engagement, engaging in lobbying, or protesting controversial bills that they believe would be harmful to their communities. At the extreme, communities might take up an alternative ethic entirely, choosing to be like the Bruderhof Community, in which members live under a rule that forsakes private ownership.

In the last several years, books like Robert D. Lupton's *Toxic Charity* and Steve Corbett's and Brian Fikkert's *When Helping Hurts* have launched much-needed reflections on how much we actually accomplish through our charitable actions.

It is beyond my ability to enter into a debate about whether these various tactics are immoral or unhelpful, ineffectual, or just wrong. Congregations will need to ask those questions in the context of their own community, armed with the desire to reveal the Kingdom of God and a deep sense of the strengths and needs of the community they serve. Rather than make those arguments, I want to explore a set of tensions that congregations will need to—and absolutely should—contend with as they begin the work of community and economic development.

These tensions fall into three general categories. The first explores the tension between charity and justice, and the role of the church in both. The second looks at the role of relationship in incarnational ministry. The final one explores how churches contend with the always-present tension between theological reflection and practice. Ultimately, we find that our framework for evangelism, and its historical precedents, helps us to navigate these tensions in ways that are responsible both theologically and practically.

CHARITY VERSUS JUSTICE

Perhaps the strongest tension in community development and community engagement is that of the tension between charity and justice. This tension arises out of a clear desire to address an ongoing challenge in the community, but unsure of the right process by which to engage. On the one hand, churches might opt to engage with charity, a response to the immediate needs of the community. On the other hand, the church might want to engage as part of a desire to see justice, which requires some political reorganization within the community.

Pope Benedict XVI's encyclical *Deus Caritas Est* discusses these alternative approaches. Charity, Benedict tells us, is "first of all the simple response to immediate needs and specific situations: feeding the hungry, clothing the naked, caring for and healing the sick, visiting those in prison."[1] This work is rooted first and foremost in an outpouring of love. Importantly, this outpouring of love is not meant as an explicit or direct means by which one reshapes society. Rather than focusing on reshaping society, the charitable action attempts to provide relief to an immediate problem. If people need food, the charitable thing to do is to feed them.

There is an obvious and strong imperative for this work in both scripture and tradition. In Matthew 25, for instance, Jesus inexorably bounds salvation with charitable actions, telling his followers that to ignore those who are hungry, naked, sick, or in prison is to ignore Jesus himself.[2] Drawing from scripture, John Wesley emphasized works of mercy within his General Rules, which were offered for early Methodists as a means of "nurturing and reshaping their character into Christ-likeness.[3]

According to Benedict, charity is part of the threefold responsibility of the church, with the other two being the proclamation of God's word and the celebration of the sacraments. The three are permanently bound together, and intrinsic in the nature of the church.[4] It is an outpouring of love, reflecting the same outpouring of love offered to us by God.

Still, while charity clearly has a scriptural and theological mandate, it does not resolve the underlying problems, meaning that the need for charity will continue. A popular metaphor for this dichotomy is discovering a steady stream of trash in a river. The practice of charity is akin to standing on the bank of the river, plucking as much trash as possible while it floats by. Still, the source of the trash is unknown. Justice, meanwhile, would be walking upstream to discover and stop the flow of trash from entering the river at all.

Justice inherently requires a reordering of society so that the underlying causes are eradicated. For Benedict, this is not the responsibility of the church, but rather the responsibility of politics, which is wholly concerned with shaping and forming our government and laws. Ideally, justice is the goal of politics, and the state is tasked with the questions of how justice should be applied.[5]

Importantly, for Benedict, the church is not meant to be entirely apart from the political world. Instead, the church is meant to help form the disciples that lead that political restructuring. After all, the church is the one who teaches what justice is; namely, that it is grounded in the realities of Jesus Christ. Rather than saying that justice is not the work of the church, one might say that justice is not a practice of the church. The church is meant to define and teach what justice is to her members, and they are in turn meant to structure society so that our societal laws and practices resemble that definition of justice.[6]

While Benedict maintains that justice is not the work of the church, though, other theologians have argued that it should be the largest, if not the sole, focus of the church. After all, justice is clearly an issue raised in scripture, about which both the early church and the people of Israel must reflect. One only needs to read the works of the prophets in the Old Testament, or Mary's song in Luke 1 to see that justice and faith are deeply connected.

Given scripture's emphasis on justice, it is not surprising that many congregations highlight the necessity of justice-oriented work. Ryan Kuja, who has a long background in international missions, argues that charity has no place in the church. For him, justice is rooted in the essence of the incarnation. Just like Jesus was radically engaged with reshaping society, Kuja argues that we in the church should be likewise engaged. In a just society, Kuja posits, there would be no need for charity, and so our work should be singularly focused on achieving that dream.

Kuja creates an analogy: if justice is the natural output of Jesus's incarnation, then charity is reminiscent of Santa Claus, designed to give out gifts to those with less. Kuja concludes quite starkly: "Biblical justice has to do with Jesus. Charity has to do with Santa Claus. And these is no such thing as charity in the kingdom of God."[7]

Such a stark position raises many questions: Is charity actually contributing to brokenness? Is it a perpetuation of unjust systems, whereby the wealthy give to the poor? Or can charity actually lead to justice?

In some churches, the line between those who provide charity and those who need charity is precariously thin. I have served with congregants who could just as easily receive food from the food distribution center where they volunteered. Are these really an example of injustice in my congregation's work? Or might it be a symbol of God's redeeming work in the world, a tangible display of Christian solidarity?

In practice, navigating the tension between charity and justice is quite difficult for most churches. Churches can readily see the need for charity around them, when people come to the parish asking for help with utility payments, food, or school supplies. And whether Benedict is correct or not about justice being the work of the state, it is true that churches have seemingly few avenues by which to reorder society. Churches cannot, for instance, rewrite the tax code, create laws, or reform government agencies. And where churches in past decades might have launched universities and hospitals, the small-membership church can often not afford to navigate the complex legal requirements that these endeavors would demand. This isn't to say that churches have no avenues to help create a just society—churches might launch protests, lobby lawmakers, or even create programs that help renarrate what a just society might look like.[8] Churches might find creative means to pursue justice, partnering with local hospitals to provide more access to healthcare, for instance. Even still, the small-membership congregation, *on its own,* can often gesture to a just society by beginning with works of charity and building upon them, rather than act without engaging in the work of charity at all.

Benedict rightly points out that justice needs a central definition, which is found in the nature and being of Jesus Christ.[9] In practice, church members' conception of justice is usually shaped by multiple streams of thought. In a highly polarized society, political identity, family traditions, personal experiences, and community understandings are all likely to shape what "justice" looks like. This makes understanding justice a difficult endeavor. In this case, charity—and charitable missions—might actually be a way of entering into conversations about the nature of justice as it relates to scripture. Without that formational work, though, the pursuit of justice might be unintelligible and in fact detrimental to the church community.

Several years ago, a colleague of mine served a church in a community built around a coal-powered electrical plant. The plant was quite literally at the center of the community, and the church was a short stroll from the plant's gates. For decades, the plant had been the major economic driver for the community. Members of the community would tell stories about coal ash falling like snow while they played outside.

Over the years, the coal ash was stored in unlined pits. Over time, contaminates from the coal ash had seeped into the groundwater, and it was discovered that the groundwater had high traces of dangerous materials. The well-water that most communities used was not safe for consumption, and residents were now given pallets of bottled water to drink.

The story unfolded predictably. The energy company maintained that they were not responsible for the contaminated water, environmental groups launched lawsuits, and the community became embroiled in controversy.

At the time, I was working for a university think-tank, and so at the pastor's invitation, I convened a meeting with our agency's environmental policy expert, a clean water advocate, and the pastor. The church had been invited to participate in a class-action suit against the company.

The community was divided. The company that ran the plant had been at the center of another scandal, when a major river had been contaminated by a coal ash spill. The sitting governor had close connections to the company and was accused of using his power to protect the company. The environmental scandal was wrapped in politics. Those who wanted to join the class-action suit highlighted the egregious environmental record of the company. The community members opposed to it suggested that the lawsuit was a means by which to target the then-governor. The church was unsure of what steps to take, but did not feel that they could do nothing.

As we talked, there seemed to be two different options for engagement. On the one hand, the church could take up the work of charity—distributing water and serving as a clearinghouse for information to help the wider community. On the other hand, the pastor could lead his church to participate in the lawsuit, injecting the congregation into the middle of the controversy.

The core of the dilemma was this: if the pastor took up the work of charitable action, the church would maintain a stance of nonpartiality, gain respect in the wider community, positioning the church to do more good work in the future. If the church joined in the pursuit of legal justice, it was certain they would alienate members of the congregation and the small community, jeopardizing the trust given to the church.

The tension is obvious. A justice-oriented approach offers restructuring, but at significant cost to the congregation's ministries, and very little chance for formative conversations with members, with an unclear outcome. A charitable approach provides services and goods, maintaining the relationships, helping members, but avoiding the resolution. There is no immediate and logical "correct" choice between simply choosing to do justice and choosing to do charity.

In many cases, there is no bifurcation between justice and charity; rather, the two are on a spectrum. Choosing charitable actions can be a formational step toward justice, helping the congregation understand the necessity of justice-oriented work. Meanwhile, lingering in charity might prevent the congregation from fully engaging in the life of the community. Jumping straight to works of "justice," particularly those actions that are more political in nature, might alienate members who do not hold a common understanding of justice. Churches must learn to navigate this tension in a way that helps their congregations step toward community leadership, both avoiding the temptation to not fill the potential of the church as a community anchor institution, and the temptation to build without the foundation of a common theological language.

BEING WITH OR DOING FOR?

For the church to seize upon their role as community leaders, relationships are vital. These relationships are formed in a myriad of ways. In the rural churches that I serve and work with, relationships between the church and the community are often informal. I have had a great many pastoral care and church strategy conversations in the aisle at the grocery store, while dropping my daughter off at daycare, or when I take out the trash and see a neighbor on their evening walk. Building relationships within the community is essential, and something that most congregations implicitly understand.

In the work of community development, the tension is not whether relationships are important. They are. Rather, the tension is found in the ways that churches engage with people who are not strategic partners. How do we form relationships with those whom we are serving? And, if we're not building relationships with those individuals, are we following the incarnational example of Jesus Christ well? At the same time, if all of our time is spent cultivating relationships, are we going to be able to accomplish the goals that we set out to accomplish? Or will we render our churches as social organizations that do little good in the world, other than fostering places of conversation?

In his book *A Nazareth Manifesto*, Sam Wells offers four categories of relationships for churches engaged in the community. To illustrate these, Wells uses the example of encountering a homeless person. If you are *working for* that homeless person, you join boards and agencies and advocate for her. To *work with* a homeless individual is to engage her in the work that you do, essentially asking that person to be a partner. *Being with* does not focus on the work at all, but rather focuses on building a relationship that might (or might not) change and affect you. Finally, *being for* is devoid of personal interaction. Rather, Wells describes this as seeing an issue at a distance. You might read about homelessness in the newspaper, be moved by the what you read, and begin advocacy work, ensuring that people do not make false assumptions about the homeless, regarding their life choices or personal histories, or raising money for homeless shelters in your area.[10]

One summer, my congregation was approached by a nearby food bank to become a distribution point for their summer feeding program. Every other week, we would distribute enough food for each child in qualifying families to have enough meals to last two weeks. We would provide food to roughly fifty families, many of whom had two or three children. The whole process was well organized. The families would sign in to receive a card that indicated how many children would be receiving food, and volunteers would distribute the appropriate amount of food to them. From start to finish, it took about ten minutes for a family to receive their meals. We did not know the families, and given the expedited nature of the service, we did not have a chance to get to know them. Additionally, a majority of the families were Spanish speaking, and my small congregation had only one Spanish speaker.

There are clear benefits to this type of program, which can have positive ripple effects, since hunger is related to a myriad of other health and economic problems. Our congregation was able to quickly and positively impact our community, even with our limited resources. Our relationship, though, was one based upon giving and receiving. We were, as Sam Wells would say, *working for* them. We had no serious relationship, other than recognizing an issue and moving to provide relief. How were we to build upon that work in a meaningful way, cultivating the Kingdom of God, without any sort of ongoing interaction? How would we announce and invite the community into the Kingdom of God without a deeper relationship?

Not all charitable community development work can be categorized in this *working for* relationship. I was once part of a conversation about mental healthcare in a rural community near the coast of North Carolina. This particular community had a large refugee population, and in recent months, had been scarred by a horrible triple homicide. The offender was a refugee who was left untreated for mental health and behavioral issues including posttraumatic stress disorder. Aware of the need for adequate mental healthcare in transitioning to a new community, a working group was established. Members of the group included pastors whose churches were comprised of refugees, members of the refugee community, and others who were simply passionate about this cause. The resulting actions were a partnership between the members of the refugee community and a majority white population, illustrating what Wells would identify as *working with*. This partnership sought to develop cultural competency among the predominantly white participants, develop ongoing parenting classes that aided refugees in navigating school registration for their children, doctor appointments, and other skills needed to thrive in a southern rural community.

The relationships between leaders were formed more out of utilitarian necessity than desire for friendship. Additionally, the increased number of stakeholders resulted in a slower deliberation and action, which increased the possibility of frustration among more action-oriented group members. Still, the relationships, over time, morphed into meaningful friendships. And, while the work was slow, it was intentional and worthwhile, launching a sustainable ministry that has changed both the congregations involved and the wider community.

While *doing with* still focuses on results, what Wells refers to as *being with* might have no real output other than forming a relationship. A church where my wife interned led a program that brought at-risk students together for two days each week during the summer. The aim of the program was a fairly simple one; it simply sought to provide community for the students. According to their pastor, they "spent most of the first week teaching them not to drop the f-bomb in the sanctuary, and the rest is just supposed to be sort of fun." They played games, went to the pool, or went hiking and rafting.

When I was visiting one day, the participants were doing a fairly simple activity. A facilitator paired everyone off, and the partners shared personal stories. When we came back together as a large group, each pair would tell their stories to the whole room, but with a twist: I would tell my partner's story from a first-person point of view. I would tell their story as if it were my own. And in turn, they would tell mine.

It's a deeply personal exercise. You find yourself listening intently to the other person's story, full of the responsibility of handling whatever they tell you. You find yourself trying to assure them that they are heard, understanding that they are entrusting you with something valuable. Meanwhile, as you recite your story for them to later tell, you look for every indication that you are being heard, that they value your story, as well.

As you would expect in a room full of middle schoolers, some of the stories were trivial and silly. Some were wise. Some were deep and painful. I was paired with a young teenage girl, around thirteen years old. Slowly and tearfully, she told me about the time she was violently sexually assaulted a year or two before.

I was familiar with this community, and I could easily quantify the data about poverty, drug use, violence, and inadequate health care and how those impact a child's life. As I listened to her story, and as I retold her story, that emphasis on statistics melted away. Her story, and the importance of her story, reshaped how I viewed antipoverty work. Rather than seeing her community as a dataset, I learned to recognize her as a beloved child of God. Behind each data point is an individual, who bears God's image, with their own story of pain, loss, redemption, and hope.

The exercise did nothing to eradicate poverty, or end drug abuse, or stop domestic violence. Rather, it focused on building relationships, on highlighting the incarnational presence the church can have. It was a reminder to the students, "We will hear you and believe you."

This type of work, where friendship and presence are valued above quantifiable outputs, is both impressive and deeply frustrating. We connect to the individual stories of the people who want to help, but it also leaves us wanting the world to be changed *now*. It leads us to remember and see humanity in such a way that honors each person as a unique and important creation by God. Without being bound in the story of one another, the importance of community development, particularly the church's leadership in community development, is devoid of its primary objective: to bring the wider community into the communion of God's Kingdom.

The final type of relationship that Wells describes is *being for*. A few years ago a hurricane devastated parts of the region where I grew up. The church I was serving was not impacted by the storm, but we heard stories from family members and friends, and we saw the photos of the damage to their homes and communities. My congregation decided to collect an offering to send to our denomination's relief efforts, and later decided to collect winter coats for a community that had been impacted.

We did not experience the tragedy of the storm firsthand, nor did we witness for ourselves the needs of those who had. Rather, we heard secondhand reports, and relying on those reports, began advocating for those communities through our donations and collections.

There are benefits to this: hearing that help was needed, we worked to provide it, moved by compassion and generosity. We were able to respond quickly, and we listened to those who knew better to tell us how to best help. This is not always the case, though. At times, those removed from the situation seek to provide help that is not actually needed. One need only think about the well-intentioned retiree who donates old furniture to the church's youth group to realize that, while intentions are good, they are often misguided.

For Wells, the incarnational relationship described as *being with* is an opportunity to rethink the conventions of community leadership. Rather than begin with an end goal in mind, it begins with a recognition of the person. The other three types of relationship are well-intentioned, but miss the mark of what Jesus desires for us. Wells posits that this incarnational relationship moves the work of community development past the economic dimensions, and past the tension of charity and justice, and into something that transcends both. It may involve charity from time to time, and the emphasis on relationship will transform how we conceive of our political and social systems. So, for Wells, the church should strive to *be with* more.[11]

It is true that relationships are essential in the work of community leadership. The church that wants to invite the wider community to participate in God's Kingdom must in fact know who they are inviting. That is a key part of the recognition in the previous chapter. It is also true that some relationships are healthier than others. The Kingdom of God's ultimate reality is that of a relationship between the God and creation.

Yet, churches will necessarily need to navigate the tension of when relationships ought to be built, and when action is a responsibility. It is impossible in every situation to be in a relationship with every person with whom one wants to do ministry. For instance, my wife and I give a small amount each year to our college to buy textbooks for first-generation college students. It is impossible for us to form a deep relationship with every student that might utilize those funds.

At the same time, churches should be mindful of how relationships might reframe their work. Our small donation is important to us precisely because we have known first-generation students on our campus. Building relationships is a vital piece of knowing how to lead in the community, and this work should be a priority. Yet, it should serve as a guide to the broader work of the church, not as a detraction from leading such work.

THEOLOGY AND PRACTICE

Early on in my ministry, people asked me whether I was more interested in being an academic or a pastor. Or, as one person put it, "Is your faith in the theology in your mind or in the fire in your heart?" The far-too-pervasive way of thinking is that theologians and practitioners are different breeds, with different skillsets and different passions. To some extent, this is not entirely wrong. I know a great many brilliant minds who would flounder in the local church. I know a great many pastoral minds who lead with grounded, but limited, theological reflection.

For many churches, the dichotomy is very real. Many of the churches I've visited with will tell me about a pastor who possessed a keen theological mind, but whose sermons were never quite applicable to the daily lives of those in the pews. Likewise, when it came time for a decision, the pastor would lead the church through endless theological reflection, effectively stifling any momentum. At the same time, I've sat in churches whose pastors were deemed "highly effective," but whose sermons could be reduced to a bumper sticker, and whose programs were hardly ever shaped by the theology the church claimed to profess.

This tension between practical effectiveness and theological reflection is also deeply embedded in the church's work of community development. As I mentioned in the previous chapter, some congregations will simply seek to "do good" without any serious theological reflection, eager to see results.

A Wesleyan approach to evangelism like the one outlined in the previous chapter must inherently navigate this tension. If the Kingdom of God is in fact being revealed, then how should we envision that community in practice? This requires a great deal of theological discernment. Meanwhile, such an evangelism is not called to a monastic life of contemplation. It is designed to be lived out so that it shapes our communities in meaningful ways.

One of the challenges in this is that our perceptions of action are formed in multiple spaces. Moral imaginations are shaped not just in the church because most people do not live their lives solely within the sphere of the church. As John E. Senior correctly notes,

> Persons learn how to be customers when they participate in the marketplace, soldiers when they participate in the military, citizens when they participate in political life, children of God when they participate in faith communities, and so on . . . person are formed in multiple ways in multiple institutional settings.[12]

Each of these settings forms us to see the world in a particular way. For instance, we perceive it as "good" when companies offer high-quality products for low cost, and so we believe that stores and corporations are acting morally when they are able to "look out for the customer." Meanwhile, in business, we are taught to maximize profitability, and so it is a moral good to be able to earn a decent living. Those with military or government service see patriotism as a value in a different way than those of us who might not have served. Parents teach lessons about what is and is not correct behavior, or about how to behave in relationships, which their kids carry into adulthood and pass on.

Importantly, these spaces do not always create value systems that align well. A family on a budget might believe that food, like chicken, needs to be affordable to feed their family, a belief formed through the marketplace. And, they might also believe that farms should be sustainable, and that the farmers should be well compensated, beliefs formed by a political and/or a theological conviction. These two beliefs might not necessarily align, as larger companies are able to expedite production, but at a loss for environmental sustainability and by shifting the liabilities of production to the farmer.

Because people have been formed in multiple spaces with different moral imaginations, our efforts in the church can reflect this ambiguity. The church's community leadership, particularly work in community development, can easily be swayed by the definitions of justice or morality from other avenues. Before embarking on community and economic development initiatives, churches should be clear about where their moral vision for the community is being formed.

When it comes to economic development, this focus on a moral vision is sometimes second to conversations about the economy itself. A few years ago, I attended a conference that focused on early childhood development. The speakers mentioned that, in order to help the economy of our state, we needed to produce students who could fulfill particular jobs. With that in mind, we should be promoting and funding more classes and avenues to those careers. By doing this, we could ensure a vibrant economy in the future.

On the surface, there is nothing wrong with this conclusion: we want a strong economy for our society, and therefore we should train students to fill necessary jobs in that society. In fact, it seems laudable. But in digging deeper, we quickly realize that what is valued here is a vague description of "the economy," in which our ultimate goal is ensuring a "strong economy," defined differently by each individual. The person working to create the economy, in this equation, is less valuable than the economy that they produce. So the God-given passions, talents, and fullness of life are seen as perfunctory rather than essential. Rather than develop an economy that seeks to help students flourish postgraduation, we were forming a moral vision wherein the students only saw themselves as part of a toolkit.

In such a scenario, it is clear that our moral vision is formed by our ideals about economics and jobs. As D. Stephen Long argues, this can be incongruous with parts of our Christian tradition, undermining our beliefs about the current presence of Kingdom of God and what God teaches us about our own humanity through the incarnation of Christ and his death and resurrection. Instead, this notion of the individual as a part of a larger economic toolkit actually can reshape our understanding of who Jesus is, and what God desires for us. Instead of our theology shaping how we view the world, our view of the world, in this case, shapes our theology.[13]

None of this is necessarily nefarious, and often presents itself in fairly innocuous ways. For instance, in chapter 2, we noted that the prevailing metrics used to evaluate church vitality, namely Average Worship Attendance, are borrowed from popular business leadership practices, often with little theological reflection. In turn, this has shaped our views of what it means to practice evangelism. Or consider how many people see their Christian faith as a means by which to avoid punishment for the lives we lead, rather than a way by which we encounter a relationship with the living God, and in doing so, uncover a new way of living for ourselves.

If the church is to assume the mantle of community leadership, it is imperative that we give theology the task of "evaluating the ends of all other discourses."[14] Theology needs to be the foundational point from which we build our community development efforts. We need to be focused on our theological goals: announcing and inviting the wider community into the Kingdom of God.

The hardship, here, is that this theological reflection on its own gives us no real practices by which to achieve that. In order to do that, various theologians, practitioners, and ethicists have offered practices that help point toward some way of church leadership for the wider community. The work of sanctification, after all, requires some sort of practice; it is the responsibility that we have to respond to God's grace.

The challenge in these theologies is that their end goal, the *telos*, must still remain grounded in a clear theological vision. This is not an easy task, given the multiple ways that our imaginations have been formed. The work of community development and community leadership has a public face, and involves interacting with those stakeholders and agencies that have similar, but still different goals.[15] It is not the goal of the local library to invite participation into the Kingdom of God, for instance, even as they might still be meaningful partners for leading literacy programs in the county. Neither, though, does the church want to become solely focused on building literacy programs. When it comes to community and economic development, the church should be insistent that their theological convictions do not result in swapping one flawed political system for another.

Joerg Rieger has written extensively about economics and theology. Through his multiple books, Rieger has begun to articulate a practice he calls *deep solidarity*. Rieger argues that our work in economic development should resemble the incarnation. In the incarnation, God moves downward toward humanity, born as a poor baby rather than a powerful king.[16] For Rieger, this gives us a glimpse as to how the church might lead in their communities. Rather than inviting people up to God, we should mirror God's practices and move downward to participate with all members of our community.

Rieger's notion of *deep solidarity* calls us to "understand ourselves in terms of those whom we consider less fortunate."[17] Rather than viewing community development as being for the benefit of someone who is less fortunate, Rieger argues that we should recognize that we are intertwined—what happens to one person impacts the wider community, and therefore, all must be a part of the solution.[18] Certainly, this is representative of what we see in the early church, particularly in Acts 5, wherein the community was dedicated to caring for one another, even sharing resources among themselves. If scripture is any indication, there is clearly a focus on the concern of the well-being of the whole community.

Establishing such practices can also offer a means by which we journey toward sanctification, reminding us of the necessity for means of grace. If Matthew 25 is to be believed, then one way we might encounter Jesus is to visit with those who are hungry, sick, homeless, or in prison.[19] And, in practice, understanding how we are interconnected helps those of us leading community development to understand both the needs of our community, and what it means to live into the realities and presence of the Kingdom of God.

At the same time, leaning too far into such practices can warp our theological understanding of community, and mutate our end goals to be something foreign to what we initially began with. If we fuse our practices with our political formation and beliefs, for instance, our goal might mutate so that community development looks like supporting or defeating one political party. Instead of forming political opinions based upon theological principles, the theological ideals end up normed and formed by political standards. Likewise, economic development work that is built upon the criticism of our current economic system might end up advocating for a swap with another flawed, human-built economic engine. Rather than push toward a theological vision of economics, we might end up accommodating a new and flawed system within our theology.

In an extreme case, following Rieger's argument, a congregation might criticize certain facets of our capitalistic economy: it does not care enough about people, there is a wide wealth disparity, or people do not have a clear path by which to gain a job, afford healthcare, or pay for college. By diving into the practices of Rieger's *deep solidarity* without first grounding it in a theological *telos*, the congregation sees these deficiencies and opts to support an alternative economic system, such as Marxism. Rather than establishing a theological goal rooted in an understanding of salvation and scripture, a congregation might affirm that a Marxist society *is* the goal.

The danger, though, is that Marxism, like capitalism, is designed and controlled by humans, and is likewise corrupted by sin. Neither capitalism nor Marxism are themselves a theological *telos*. Rather than arrive at the Kingdom of God, such an ideology arrives at another flawed and broken system, which will in turn be reacted against. And the end result is that rather than make clear the reality of the Kingdom of God, such a process inadvertently suppresses theological convictions, replacing them with this new goal.

By leaning too far into practices without grounding ourselves in theology, we risk measuring our fruits only by what we produce, and defining ourselves by how far we are removed from the initial starting point, rather than how close we are to the Kingdom of God. In doing so, we lose sight of our initial understanding of concepts such as justice, salvation, and redemption.[20]

Likewise, when it comes to theological principles, congregations will have to navigate the tension between their theology and expediency. This can render the work of community leadership as morally ambiguous, though it need not be. In order to prevent that, churches must maintain a clear understanding of their theological identity, where what we offer to the world is substantially different from what we would produce without Jesus.

The tension, then, is navigating the weaknesses of both "theology without practice" or "practice without theology." While Long is correct that theology must be what the church uses to evaluate all other fields, that analyses is of little value unless it can guide our practices in meaningful ways. At the other end, Rieger's practices of *deep solidarity* offer a means by which we can move toward sanctification. The danger, though, is that it is easily maladapted. Without a theological *telos*, our goals can easily mutate away from the Kingdom of God, leading us no closer to a community shaped by Jesus's life, death, and resurrection.

NAVIGATING TENSIONS

In chapter 3, I outlined a process of evangelism as community development. Central to my argument is that understanding community development as evangelism can help achieve at least three meaningful goals. First, it provides a framework for rural congregations to reengage in their communities and live into our biblical mandate to make disciples. Second, it grounds our understanding of community leadership in a theological practice, ensuring that our theological convictions are foundational to what we practice. Third, it provides a way to practice evangelism, which is a necessary theological practice. Without theology, evangelism is not rightly a practice of the church. Without practice, evangelism is defunct as a theological subject.

Evangelism as community development also helps us navigate these important tensions between charity and justice, relationships, and practice and theology. It does so because it is inherently about both charity and justice, depends on forming meaningful relationships as we invite the wider community into the Kingdom of God, and maintains a meaningful focus on our soteriology, or theology of salvation.

Here again, I want to draw upon Laceye Warner's study of women in the eighteenth and nineteenth century to help understand how such work navigates these tensions, by utilizing her profile of Dorothy Ripley.

Born in England to a Methodist preacher, Ripley was raised in a deeply spiritual home.[21] Later in her life, she affirmed both a Wesleyan understanding of justification and sanctification.[22] Because God had worked in her life and in her spirit, she felt compelled to act within the wider world. This soteriology became a foundational point for her own work, as she attempted to pattern her life around Jesus's own actions, emphasizing a connection between love of God and love of neighbor.[23] Ripley was motivated in part by what she saw as a "nominal acceptance of Christianity."[24] As she traveled to the United States, she decried slavery as an example of this lukewarm faith. Her work began to take the shape of abolitionism.

Ripley spent time among enslaved peoples and intervened for them by calling slaveowners to account, a bold and dangerous act of charity for a woman in the early nineteenth century.[25] Ripley sought justice by demanding that the children of slaveowners free their slaves when they were inherited as part of their repentance and turns toward Christ. In meeting with President Thomas Jefferson, she even pressed Jefferson on his status as a slaveowner.[26]

Here we see Ripley navigating a myriad of tensions. She is engaged in both charity and justice, intervening in charitable ways while pressing for a larger societal change. She is engaged in different forms of relationships, interacting *with* slaves (and slaveowners) while also acting *for* enslaved people in places where an advocate was necessary. Finally, she is connecting practice and faith, demanding that slaveowners and their children free slaves as an act of repentance in their conversions.[27]

Importantly, Ripley's work was not just in a desire to see slavery abolished, but rather an understanding that to truly be in alignment with what God wills, slavery cannot stand. Her evangelism was in many ways holding people to account for what they claimed as a faith, which she rightly regarded as nominal. In doing so, Ripley connected evangelism with habits that allowed communities to practice the ethics of the Kingdom of God, and become habituated to a life of conversion and repentance in clear and tangible ways.

This form of evangelism maintained a clear emphasis on scripture and faith, which formed Ripley's ethical vision. Likewise, it connected practice to theology in meaningful ways, ways that cut through the tensions detailed previously in this chapter. Finally, Ripley kept a meaningful focus on conversion, not just of the spirit, but of the whole society, connecting practices of justice and economics with practices of faith and spirituality.

By reclaiming this theological practice of evangelism, rural churches can navigate these tensions that can leave churches lingering in debates, arrest their forward momentum, or cause them to drift away from their goals. Grounding their work in a practice of community development as evangelism provides a template to navigate those tensions, so that rural congregations are able to authentically and faithfully share the work of Christ in our world.

NOTES

1. Benedict XVI. "Deus Caritas Est (December 25, 2005)." *BENEDICT XVI*, 2005, w2.vatican.va/content/benedict-xvi/en/encyclicals/documents/hf_ben-xvi_enc_20051225_deus-caritas-est.html. Paragraph 31a.

2. Matthew 25:31-46.

3. Maddox, Randy L. *Responsible Grace: John Wesley's Practical Theology.* Kingswood Books, 1994. 212.

4. Benedict XVI, 25a.

5. Ibid., 26–28a.

6. Ibid., 28a.

7. Kuja, Ryan. *From the Inside Out: Reimagining Mission, Recreating the World.* Cascade Books, 2018. 55.

8. One prominent example is the number of churches creating funds to help members pay off debt. For one example, see: Grace, Joshua. "My Church Came Together to Pay Off Each Member's Debt." *Sojourners*, June 17, 2019, sojo.net/magazine/july -2019/my-church-came-together-pay-each-members-debt.

9. Benedict XVI, 28a.

10. Wells, Samuel. *A Nazareth Manifesto: Being with God.* Malden, MA: Wiley Blackwell, 2015. 11–20.

11. Ibid., 279–82.

12. Senior, John E. *Theology of Political Vocation: Christian Life and Public Office.* Baylor University Press, 2015. 50.

13. Long, D. Stephen. *Divine Economy Theology and the Market.* Taylor and Francis, 2002. 68.

14. Ibid., 2.

15. Senior, *Theology of Political Vocation*, 52–57.

16. Rieger, Joerg. *No Rising Tide: Theology, Economics, and the Future.* Fortress Press, 2009. 79–80.

17. Rieger, Joerg. "Occupy Wall Street and Everything Else: Lessons for the Study and Praxis of Religion." *Peace Studies Journal* 5, no. 10 (January 2012): 33–45.

18. Rieger, Joerg, and Pui-lan Kwok. *Occupy Religion: Theology of the Multitude.* Rowman & Littlefield, 2013. 64.

19. Matthew 25:31-46.

20. Long, *Divine Economy Theology and the Market*, 117. Long writes, "Marxism imposes 'limitations' on theology because it recognizes its socially productive character. The result is that traditional Christian theological themes will be subordinated to an overarching metaphysical liberty . . . this common theme in liberation theology will result in necessary ecclesiological and Christological limitations and finally fail to offer a significant alternative to the metaphysics of scarcity that capitalism assumes."

21. Warner, *Saving Women*, 20.

22. Ibid., 32.

23. Ibid., 35.

24. Ibid.

25. Ibid., 44.

26. Ibid., 47.

27. Ibid., 39.

Chapter 5

Reclaiming Practice

A few years ago, I was lamenting with a senior colleague and mentor that the field of evangelism is not always taken very seriously within the academy. Theology, I reasoned, should have some bearing on our practice. What excited me about the field of evangelism is that it had the potential to cut across multiple disciplines.

"It's more than that," she told me. "Theology, rightfully understood, should *be* evangelism. It should, at least in part, help us to communicate what God is doing in our world and who God is."

This conversation stuck with me. What I've attempted to outline so far in this book is a theologically grounded practice of evangelism that both enables rural churches to be more vital, while also helping to share the good news of the Gospel. My hope is that rural congregations will be able to lead within their communities, their theological identity serving as a firm foundation. Given all of that, the natural and pivotal question is this: Does this notion of community development as evangelism actually work in practice? Can we see what it looks like on the ground?

To answer that question, I want to offer three different vignettes that explore this evangelism in practice. I placed some criteria for the stories that I chose. First, all of the churches had to be small-membership. Contrary to some narratives, there are actually a number of larger rural congregations. While they do good work, I find that the stories of large membership churches are often overtold, and I think it's vitally important that we lift up and learn from small-membership churches.

The second criterion is that these churches all meet a common definition of rural. As was discussed in the first chapter, the definition of rural can be hard to pin down. In most day-to-day conversations, it is usually defined by a person's imagination of rural rather than what *is* rural. All three of these communities, then, meet the United States Department of Agriculture's (USDA) definition of rural under their Rural-Urban Communiting Area Codes.[1]

Lastly, I have tried to select case studies that demonstrate different practices. These churches are engaged in a myriad of different types of work, formed and steeped in different contexts. All three are responding to what they feel God is leading them to on the ground. This diversity of practice and program is important, I think. Too often, the temptation of the church—and many organizations—is to find a quick fix that can be borrowed wholesale from one context and placed in another. While ideas might be borrowed, they almost always need to be adapted. Neither community leadership nor evangelism can thrive if they are rooted on adopting wholesale the prescriptions from another community. Churches need to adapt for their context, rather than blindly adopt wholesale. Instead, these churches are responding to the unique needs of their own people, and in doing so, are revealing a portion of the Kingdom of God.

With those standards being set, it is prudent to offer a few caveats. The first of which is that, while I will use different communities to use as case studies, they simply cannot be representative of the whole of rural America. Such an endeavor would be impossible in only three case studies. I did endeavor, though, to find examples that could feasibly have taken place in a variety of contexts.

Second, it's worth mentioning that two of the examples are within my own denomination, The United Methodist Church. Because I am familiar with more churches in this denomination, finding churches was a simpler and more expedient task. The other church is a Missionary Baptist congregation and was selected because they are a national model for community leadership. All three churches were selected because they exhibited these practices of community development as evangelism, even if they do not explicitly name it as such themselves. Their work provides a glimpse of the power of the rural church.

Lastly, all of these churches strive, as D. Stephen Long says, to "present our gifts to God, and in doing so are not alienated from them, but we and they are taken up into God's own life. This is Christian theological economics."[2] Each of these communities is responding to a particular need, and offering a Christ-centered response to it. In doing so, they are joining with God's work. None of this, though, is perfect in its endeavors. Some critics might argue that they are perpetuating existing economic systems, that they are not going far enough, or that the work is not yet deep enough. To answer those critics, I would simply hold fast to Wesley's notion that we are on a theological journey. The people embarking on this journey in these congregations are on a path toward sanctification, and their work is a step in that long journey.

BUILDING SKILLS, BUILDING DISCIPLES

To say that Gainesboro is a small town is an understatement, boasting a population of less than 1,000. The childhood poverty rate is high, almost reaching almost 50 percent of the under-eighteen population. Sitting on a two-point charge, First United Methodist Church in Gainesboro has an average worship attendance of fifty-five, which makes them a large church compared to their sister congregation, which has less than fifteen on a Sunday morning.

Their pastor, Tim, is a licensed local pastor in The United Methodist Church, which means that Tim is not ordained, but rather licensed, to serve as a pastor. Like many licensed local pastors, Tim is second career. A former chef, he felt a call to ministry, left his career, and followed this new vocation.

The church sits in the middle of the small, nondescript downtown, surrounded by a few shops, empty buildings, and a couple of other churches. Because of its location in town, Tim has long recognized that his congregation is an anchor institution.

I met Tim when his District Superintendent recommended him to be part of a cohort I was leading, which would work with rural pastors on community leadership. Early in the process, we had the small group of pastors identify assets in their communities.

Tim's list took me a bit by surprise.

"Well," he began, "We have some angry contractors. They're upset that the kids about to graduate from high-school don't know how to swing a hammer. And we have a bunch of other high-schoolers who don't know how to swing a hammer. And we have a building that someone gave us. It needs a lot of work. Lights. Windows. A wall. But it's ours."

There was an awkward pause, as his other participants and the facilitator tried to figure out how to respond. Tim broke the silence with the story of how the building came into their possession. The congregation had been pondering how they could create a space for youth in the community. Then, someone donated this building. It was, as Tim repeated throughout our cohort, one of "those God things."

The wonderful thing about working with Tim was that he could quickly recognize all the places where God was at work around him. Tim had no trouble seeing that God's prevenient grace was already at work, ready to transform his community.

So Tim began to cultivate. He met with stakeholders: county leaders, volunteers, and church partners. Pretty soon, a plan emerged. They would launch a new youth center in the new building. Each youth would be paired with an adult. After a time of Bible study, some fun activities, and food, the adult would work with the students on a project, teaching a skill.

With a plan in place, Tim began to announce what God's grace was doing in this world. Within about six weeks, the youth center had around forty students participating. They came together for their weekly Bible study, and they learned skills in how to do electrical work, lay pavers on a walkway, and do construction work.

From an economic perspective, this is affordable and effective economic development model. The church is creating mentorships, and in doing so, offering low-cost job training for high-schoolers in the community who may not be seeking education after graduation. By forming these mentorships and social connections, the church is also creating job pipelines for these students. A contractor who has personally mentored a student in how to do a specific job, for instance, will trust the skills of his mentee.

For Tim and his parishioners, this was a theological event. The ultimate goal is to help with the faith and moral formation of a group of young people in the community. The means by which to do that, in this case, was through providing a youth center that also served as a social space for teenagers, provided personal and professional mentorship for students, and fostered cross-generational relationships.

As they announce the reign of God, Tim and his leaders are not denying the economic and social benefits of the program. Indeed, that was part of their motivation. But the motivation to foster a thriving community is intimately connected with the desire to form disciples who are leading their community. In talking to Tim, you quickly realize that the formation of discipleship is at the core of the program. They are able to articulate a clear theological vision for what they are doing.

Ultimately, Tim's youth center is beginning to invite people to participate in God's Kingdom. Whether the youth and volunteers are coming to learn to read scripture, coming to socialize and hang out, or coming to teach or learn skills that can be useful for later on, they are being shaped and formed into disciples. They are learning that the Kingdom of God has something to say about things like vocation and employment, and that ethics and moral formation matter as well. This is not happening as some sort of ulterior motive, nor is it inherently political. Tim can articulate a clear desire to help the teenagers of his community and incorporate them into the body of Christ.

Perhaps best of all is the status of the church in the community. As Tim shared with our cohort once, "The best part about this is that the county and the town are starting to see our church as the leader." The small church is becoming a vital community leader, valued for its ability to articulate a hopeful vision. In doing so, Tim is helping his congregation explore new practices of vitality.

RECOVERING FROM THE FLOODS

In the summer of 2016, floodwaters overtook portions of West Virginia. Like many rural natural disasters, the floods did not receive the same national attention as disasters in more urban areas.[3] For those in the small town of Rainelle, though, the waters were devastating.

On Thursday, June 23, 2016, the town of 1,500 found itself in the midst of a 1,000-year flood. In some places, the water crested more than seven feet, lingering from rains on Thursday afternoon until they began to recede the next Monday. Across the state of West Virginia, twenty-six people died in the flood waters; four of those deaths were in Rainelle. More than 100 homes and businesses in the small town were destroyed.[4]

The Reverend Jonathan Dierdorff had been serving as the pastor of Rainelle United Methodist Church and Bascom United Methodist Church for one year when the rains started to fall. Prior to Jonathan's tenure, the church looked to be heading towards closure. When Jonathan arrived, that decline appeared to be reversing. In his first year, Jonathan had grown the small church by more than 40 percent, increasing the worship attendance from forty-seven to eighty-one. Once, the church had struggled to pay to keep the heat on.[5] Now, the town was in crisis, and the once declining church would need to change its focus.

Natural disasters like floods are hard to overcome for organizations. If a business cannot generate revenue over too long a period, or if the costs or rehabilitating the building become too much, it may be more financially sensible to close. Churches are not dissimilar. In recessions and community disasters, as jobs leave, and the members of the congregation see a loss of income, the church will see a loss of income as well. People simply cannot give.

Fortunately, that was not the case for Jonathan's churches. Instead, the congregations became a center of the community, and as one community member described it to Jonathan, a beacon of hope.

The two churches immediately focused on the wider community, while recognizing that many of their own members were impacted by the flood. Rainelle UMC's response to the disaster began with setting up a distribution center for food and supplies. For the first critical week, the congregation was the only distribution center. During the first five weeks, the church operated on fourteen-hour days. Their sister church, Bascom UMC, became a Red Cross shelter, housing those who had lost their homes.

As I've pointed out earlier in the book, rural churches are unique in that they have deep connections to their local communities. Rainelle UMC, for instance, counted the mayor among its members. And, Rainelle formed an ecumenical ministerial association, linking the resources and networks of the American Baptist, Church of God, and the Catholic congregations.

As the church moved from response to recovery, the church was instrumental in establishing a long-term distribution site, and they began to shift their focus to helping rebuild the community. Rainelle UMC became a hotbed of activity. They received a shower truck through the denominational resources of The United Methodist Church, which enabled them to begin hosting work camps. Partnering with their district, they were able to build two bathrooms in their church facilities, each with two showers. Over the course of three years, the small church hosted over 200 work teams.

The congregation raised more than $50,000 in donations and established a plan for helping to rebuild the community. Each church would have a different responsibility in the community rebuilding process; Rainelle UMC would become the sheetrock and insulation church. To help strengthen the local economy, they bought their supplies from a local hardware store.

On the surface, none of this immediately looks like evangelism. But consider the process through which Jonathan led his churches. First, the congregation had to recognize where God was at work. In this instance, they saw an immediate need to be involved in the response and recovery of a major flood. They also recognized that they had certain resources. For starters, they recognized that their church was on higher ground than other places in the community, and that they had space and volunteers.

The two small congregations began to cultivate those resources. They worked with partners to establish their church buildings as a shelter and distribution center. They opened a conversation with the mayor, a parishioner in the congregation. They formed an ecumenical group that partnered to lead real change. Later, they welcomed work teams from across the nation, and instituted practices to help rebuild their community.

As they began their work, they began to announce the Kingdom of God, both to themselves and to the wider community. According to Jonathan, this event helped shift the perspective of the church, as the congregation inaugurated a missional mindset that would continue. They began to see that living in the Kingdom of God necessitates a community focus.

Finally, they began inviting the wider community to participate in that Kingdom. As Jonathan shared, the community recognized the church as a catalyst for good. "It took away anyone's capacity to criticize the church," he said. The church that was once on a path toward closure was now a vibrant center of community hope.

GROWING A COMMUNITY

I met Richard Joyner when I was a kid. My father ran a homeless shelter in Rocky Mount, NC, and Richard was one of the community pastors with whom my dad regularly partnered for community development initiatives. Richard also served as the chaplain at the local hospital. He was and is a respected member of the community.

As a pastor, Richard served a not-large Missionary Baptist congregation in Conetoe, North Carolina (pronounced Kah-Nee-Tah). The town of 300 is 10 miles from the nearest grocery store, which means it is located in what is known as a food desert. While there are multiple ways to define a food desert, generally, these are areas with little access to a grocery store that serves healthy food options, like fresh fruits and vegetables.[6] There, Richard launched a youth ministry that is literally growing an economy.

Whenever Richard tells the story, it tends to start in the same place. One year, Richard presided at thirty funerals. For the most part, these were preventable deaths: people were dying from high blood pressure, diabetes, and heart disease.

Looking out at the community, it was fairly easy to spot the culprit. Conetoe is only about thirty minutes from the house where I grew up. A good church supper in our part of the world is not always the healthiest event—fried vegetables, green-beans cooked with ham or bacon, loads of fried meats, all slathered in butter. Sweat tea, which can occasionally border on a sugary syrup, is sometimes the only available beverage option. Delicious though it may be, it is not healthy.

In communities with limited access to fresh fruits and vegetables, the meals are even worse. Canned vegetables often have higher amounts of sugar and sodium, and junk food sold at convenience stores might be the most widely available food. It's not hard to see why health problems were a silent and potent killer.

Seeing all of this, Richard launched a summer camp for children, where they would exercise and garden in a small plot of land. At the end of the day, the kids would take their food back home. Eventually, Richard reasoned, the kids would take the lessons back to their parents.

The summer camp was a success, and it began to grow rapidly. Initially, the "community garden" was a small plot next to the church. Pretty soon, Richard and his church found themselves opening a 25-acre garden.

The focus of the garden is twofold. First, it's about helping the wider community become healthier. But more than that, it's about empowering the next generation of leaders for the community. Youth in the community are the primary drivers of the work.

The youth-leaders decide what to plant, and then they plant and harvest everything. They do market research and negotiate prices to sell to nearby restaurants and grocers in the county. They make business decisions about how to expand their markets and services. In one instance, the youth decided that they should keep bees on site. After the youth outvoted

Richard, a volunteer donated a colony, which was placed on converted school bus, and several students became certified as beekeepers. They now produce honey sold at farmers' markets and onsite. The bees also pollinate the garden. Other farms will also rent out the bus to pollinate their crops, as well.

The garden has fundamentally changed the community. The people are healthier, more kids are graduating high-school and going into college, and the youth are empowered as leaders in their community.[7]

All of this work began when Richard recognized how God was already at work. As Richard told *Faith and Leadership*, an online magazine published by Duke University, "We have to reframe poverty. When the system talks about poverty, they start from what you don't have. If you start from what I don't have, you can't help me build on what I do have."[8]

Implicitly, Richard recognized the gifts that God had already given to the community—the wisdom of their youth, the bounty of the land, and the trusted status of the church. Even as he averaged more than two funerals a month, Richard saw that God was at work.

Pulling together all of these resources, Richard began cultivating the Kingdom of God. Pulling together partners from throughout his community, volunteers, church members, and the teenagers in his church, Richard formulated a plan to help the community become healthier.

They would, quite literally, cultivate the soil that surrounded them. Importantly, Richard did not start with the adults, but understood that his best avenue was to work with kids. On the surface, it might seem indirect, but it was the avenue most available for him.

As the project took shape, Richard and his congregation members have heralded the Kingdom of God. They are adamant that this is part of their discipleship. To quote Richard, "Spirituality is not complete until it reaches the whole person."[9] The goal is to make a healthier community and to empower youth, yes, but the underlying goal is to help the community realize who they are in the midst of God's Kingdom.

As the project has gained a national spotlight, Richard has invited his community and the nation to join in with the Kingdom of God. They are inviting the wider community to reclaim a vital part of their faith, which is connected to practice. The garden is a place of healing and growth. It is making the community healthier, but it is also providing a spiritual balm. In an interview with CNN, Richard said, "Working in the garden has been a healing place . . . It's a place we can play. It's a place where we can produce. And it's a place where we can live."[10]

The work of Conetoe Missionary Baptist Church has quite literally grown an economy. It is an economy that values and promotes health, provides opportunities, and cultivates vocation and fulfillment. In growing that garden, they are promoting a tangible vision of the Kingdom of God, where all can find a place to live well.

RECLAIMING COMMUNITY

I chose these three examples because I wanted to demonstrate that the theology of evangelism that I have argued for is one that is inherently practical. It lives and moves, and is best understood when it is seen in the local community.

While none of these pastors necessarily articulate their work through this fourfold practice of evangelism that I have presented, it is readily apparent. They are all living into and responding to the grace that they see around them, helping their communities recognize how God is moving to create something new.

In addition to this fourfold pattern, each of these congregations has a few other similarities that I think are worth mentioning here. First, each congregation is responding to their immediate context. In politicized world, there is a tendency to follow national political conversations. These congregations do not necessarily ignore the wider conversations of our culture. Neither are they superimposing them onto their communities, though. They are responding to what is happening on the ground.

In the same way, the congregations are not adopting programs or mission tactics that they found in a list of "best practices." They did not set out looking for a silver bullet. Instead, they utilized the resources that were in front of them and found creative ways to solve problems.

Second, all three of these congregations lead from a place of theological conviction. Tim's work, for instance, began as an idea for a youth center and steadily morphed. Jonathan shared stories of baptisms following his church's work in the community. Richard wants to connect spirituality to health and economic vitality. Their theological convictions are not something that need to be sheltered away to invite partners or increase their ability to work. Their social work and beliefs can stand side by side and need no accommodation.

Third, all of these leaders see their work as the beginning, not the end. In Wesleyan theology, sanctification can, and usually does, take a life time. These churches have recognized that their work is not going to immediately solve every problem. By understanding that they are on a journey, they open themselves up to confront new challenges, to adapt and mold, and to reflect theologically upon their work often. They are able to perfect their theologies as they themselves grow in a life of discipleship. And, they are able to invite the wider community to join that growth as well.

These churches are not large or prosperous. Neither are the communities where they sit. But, they are demonstrating what it means to be a church and an anchor institution, to lead a community to a new vision, and offer hope in life-giving ways. These churches are reclaiming the gift of rural.

NOTES

1. See chapter 1, endnote 2.
2. Long, *Divine Economy Theology and the Market*, 268.
3. This phenomenon has been explored in multiple places. For a more recent example, see House, Silas. "Eastern Kentucky Has Been Underwater, but You Probably Didn't Notice." *The Atlantic, Atlantic Media Company*, February 23, 2020, www.theatlantic.com/ideas/archive/2020/02/eastern-kentucky-is-underwater-but-you-probably-didnt-notice/606973/.
4. Skinner, Jennifer. "If There's Another Flood, 'I Certainly Won't Wait for Anybody to Call Me. I'll Just Come Down, Start Paddling'." *100 Days in Appalachia*, September 27, 2017, www.100daysinappalachia.com/2017/06/rainelle-flood-2016-resucers-remember/.
5. Dierdorff, Jonathan, and Allen Stanton. "Interview with Jonathan Dierdorff." March 3, 2020.
6. "Documentation." USDA ERS—Documentation, United States Department of Agriculture —Economic Research Service, October 31, 2019, www.ers.usda.gov/data-products/food-access-research-atlas/documentation/.
7. Toner, Kathleen. "'By Nourishing Plants, You're Nourishing Community'." *CNN, Cable News Network*, March 21, 2016, www.cnn.com/2015/09/24/us/cnn-heroes-joyner/index.html.
8. Lacy, Bridgette A. "A Community Grows Its Way out of Poverty." *Faith and Leadership*, October 6, 2015, faithandleadership.com/community-grows-its-way-out-poverty.
9. Ibid.
10. Toner, "By Nourishing Plants, You're Nourishing Community."

Chapter 6

Reclaiming a Future

Not infrequently, I find myself in a room of well-intentioned church leaders, discussing the types of things that well-intentioned church leaders tend to discuss. We talk about creating leadership opportunities for the laity and strengthening our clergy's leadership capacity. We emphasize the importance of adaptive leadership and emotional intelligence. All of this is aimed at a wider conversation about the vitality of churches.

These conversations tend to be unfortunately dichotomous. To hold up the image of a thriving church as an exemplar is to simultaneously imagine a nonvital church. The vital church must reflect certain prescriptive practices. These practices are formed through a social memory of success, crafted in our more affluent urban and suburban cultures. If nonvital churches want to resemble these churches, they must adopt the prescriptive practices.

At some point in this conversation about vitality, a colleague will turn to ask me some form of the same question: "Do you really believe that there is a future for these small, rural congregations?"

This question, and the dichotomous view of vitality it assumes, stems from a lack of imagination. My answer to that question is always a resounding yes. I believe that the rural church can have a vibrant and hopeful future. And, I believe that for the sake of the communities in which they are located, the rural church must be allowed to thrive. As one of a few anchor institutions, the rural church must thrive in order to help the wider community thrive.

That I believe all of this should not be a surprise; it is the undercurrent of this book. Yet, I am also under no illusions that every rural congregation will be able to live into vitality, or that ecclesial systems are always in place to support such efforts.

In this chapter, I want to nuance that hope slightly. In order to seize this vision of evangelism and community leadership, the rural church, and those who lead our churches and their denominational structures, will need to help ground some wider institutional practices to help that vitality emerge. As the rural church begins to reclaim its identity as anchor institution, there are two practices that are especially important. First and foremost is the recruitment of pastors to rural communities. Both wider denominational systems and local churches need to think deeply about the underlying assumptions they have for rural church leaders. The second is the necessity for both denominational and local systems to develop systems of accountability that can better assess the work of the rural church. While neither of these will save the rural church, they will, I believe, make room for the rural church to reclaim her place within the wider landscape of community leadership and evangelism.

RECRUITING PASTORS

When I was a seminarian, it wasn't uncommon for a classmate to transfer out of the three-year Master of Divinity degree and instead complete one of the shorter Master of Arts degrees. When asked about their decision, they often remarked, "I just want to get into ministry faster."

This type of response is revealing. For church "professionals" the idea of a career in ministry is usually limited to a call to ordination. To be an ordained person in most mainline denominations entails not only a sense of call, but a commitment of time, money, and patience to navigate the academic and bureaucratic hoops necessary to achieve ordination. Even in churches without strict ordination requirements, the expectation of three years of seminary post-undergraduate is a financial commitment that should not be entered into lightly.

My classmates who mentioned "getting into ministry" faster were noting that their call to ministry might not actually be in on an ordination track. In turn, this means that these classmates saw their ministry as not necessarily located in a congregational setting.

This anecdotal reality plays out in data, as well. Since 2001, only about one-third of all seminarians go on to serve a local congregation.[1] Where once seminarians were largely called to the task of shepherding, theological students are now living out their vocations in unique ways, such as through nonprofit work, social justice, and missions. The goal of seminary and theological education is not necessarily to lead a congregation, but more as an avenue by which they might be able to lead change in the world. Elaine Heath, a professor of evangelism and former seminary dean, noticed this trend in her own students. While at Perkins School of Theology at Southern Methodist University, Heath launched multiple missional communities with students. She started the communities because she noticed that they were seeking a path to ministry that was entrenched in the traditions of the church, that was deeply theological, and yet not necessarily in the traditional congregational ministry. In her words,

> The communities began as learning initiatives that I started with some of my students who felt called to do ministry beyond the walls of the church but still connected to the institutional church. They felt called to go and do something entrepreneurial out in the city, where people are suffering.[2]

Importantly, this new sense of vocation cuts across ecclesial lines. In an interview with NPR, for example, one Roman Catholic seminarian recounted his sense of call as being deeply dedicated to others:

> "There's this desire, through creating obligations for myself, for doing this or that or the other, of focusing on how do I help others. It's not an active thought," he says. "And this escalated: How can I spend more time doing something for someone else rather than doing something for myself? . . . So that again kept chipping away."[3]

All of this gives way to an important and obvious question: What does this mean for those who might be called to rural ministry?

I believe that rural communities are places that can sustain this diffusion of vocational callings. But this also requires theological students learn to properly "read" their communities. Leonora Tubbs Tisdale writes that when seminaries teach preaching, they do a great disservice to their students and the churches they will serve. In a preaching course, there is ample attention paid to exegesis of the scripture. A student necessarily learns how to read scripture and draw out salient details, to know the history and context of the verses they are reading, to evaluate it through a variety of lenses, and ultimately, prepare to communicate it.

But, Tisdale notes, there is very little attention paid to the exegesis of the community. As a result, Tisdale argues, pastors often make one of three errors.[4] The first is that the sermon is for a portrait of humanity, for some generic and universal person, rather than to a specific individual. The second is that they "paint overly simplistic pictures" of their congregants. The preacher assumes that everyone shares the same emotion and assumes that everyone has had some of the same experiences. The third mistake is that the preacher projects their own biases, concerns, and issues, onto the congregation.

When seminarians are placed in small-membership, rural congregations at the beginning of their career, there is a natural idea that they will, if all goes well, grow out of that appointment. In turn, these congregations are viewed as a training ground, where the pastor can try, fail, learn, and grow.[5] When the young pastor succeeds, they relocate to a larger parish.

This cycle can be valuable. These early pastorates *should* be educational. This learning period should be intentional, though. When I was assigned to my first pastorate, a respected pastor told me that, as long as I didn't mess anything up, I would "be out and on my way within 4 years." This type of sentiment can negate the impulses to lead, to experiment, or to feel committed to the community.

If the rural church is a short stop in a longer career, the pastors that serve in these places and their denominational supervisors should guard against the temptation to do little exegetical work within the community. The assumption that this small church is a stopping point or a stepping stone allows the preacher to practice sermons and ministry techniques for future settings, rather than the setting they serve. And they can inadvertently flatten the congregation, encouraging the pastor to ignore, rather than learn, the nuances of their community. The end result is that there is a false notion of the rural community among pastors, from newly minted seminary graduates to senior pastors who are unable to talk about rural ministry with any hint of nuance.

A few years ago, I was describing my rural congregation to a senior colleague. When I finished, he politely informed me that my parish was not a "typical rural church." Hopefully, by this point, I've done a sufficient job of convincing readers that there is no such thing as a "typical rural church." Yet, these conversations persist—there is a sense among clergy that the rural church is a place without nuance, and that ministry in these settings is ultimately probationary.

Again, none of this is to say that these churches are *not* places of learning. Each stop on a ministry journey should be a place of learning and growth for the leader, and those are lessons that can be carried into their new settings of ministry as well. At the same time, it is unfair to the potential of rural congregations to see these churches as only educational pit stops for the gifted leader.

With all of that said, a pointed question remains: For seminarians and gifted leaders who want to serve a call to social justice, or missions, or evangelism, why would they choose to serve a rural parish?

The answer, obviously, is that rural churches are a place to exercise those gifts. If you want to fundamentally change the DNA of a community, help kids read at grade level by the third grade. Establish mentorship programs. Introduce conversations about vocation. Start programs that enable better practices of preventative healthcare.

The rural church is a place where these parish ministry and deep mission intersect in meaningful ways. The traditional strengths of the rural church, especially the deep relationships and sense of place, are natural assets for missional and social justice work.

One of the strengths for the rural church, of course, is its stability. As numerous scholars have highlighted, our small-membership churches tend to be long-standing institutions. Either they were established as small congregations, or they have shrunk to a sustainable equilibrium. These congregations have perpetuated themselves, proving resiliency and adaptability. Rather than cave to wider societal changes, they continue to press on. They are, as Lewis Parks aptly highlights, "a witness to the value of maintaining focus over the long run."[6]

This allows the rural church to be a natural foundation for community transformation, with a rich source of conviction, passion, and knowledge. The rural church, in that sense, is a natural place to exercise talent for missions and social justice, fully equipped assets that other nonprofits long for. They are stable, their members possess a wealth of knowledge about the community, and they have the theological rational for entering into missions.

The challenge, of course, is that the pastor and the congregation in these places might need to do some immediate heavy lifting in order to render these assets useful. If the congregation is not missional, or does not see itself as an anchor institution, then the pastor will need to cultivate a strong theological identity and imagination. This, of course, is done through the life of the church. Pastoral care is necessary to care for the congregation, yes, but also a way to exegete the community and uncover gifts. Preaching and worship are spaces where people imagine, learn, and grow. Missions, of course, become opportunities for the congregation to learn more about the realities of the Kingdom of God. In this way, the pastor of the rural church shepherds the congregation and the wider community. Rather than a place to "hang out until the next pastorate," the pastor is building a vibrant community of worship and mission.

SHAPING THE NARRATIVE

This is not a small shift in thinking, and it is further complicated by the disparate realities of rural congregations. Some small-membership congregations can afford full-time, ordained pastors with seminary educations. Attempting to attract clergy who have high amounts of student debt to low-paying congregations is setting up the church and pastor for failure. Congregations have tried to mitigate this in a variety of ways. Some congregations rely on bivocational ministers. Some congregations can afford nothing more than supply pastors. Still, denominations and congregations can both take steps to ensure more quality pastors in rural spaces.

The answer to this question, I think, is less in the recruitment of pastors, and more in how we imagine the potential of congregations and hold rural congregations accountable. This is twofold. On the one hand, denominational leaders, I believe, have a responsibility to better narrate the way we talk about rural ministry. And, congregations have a responsibility to think through their potential ministry in their contexts, while ensuring that they are holding themselves accountable.

First, church leaders should pay attention to the way that we talk about our rural congregations. I was once sent to a conference on entrepreneurship at a large research university. One speaker stood up and talked about the revenue generated by various industries. Holding up a single coin next to a jar full of coins, she pointed out that only a small percentage of companies would generate more than $1 million in revenue. "The question you need to ask yourselves is whether you want to be in this jar with all of these others, or rather you want to stand out?"

As I drove back to my small community, I thought about the numerous small businesses in my communities. Most of them existed to provide income for their families and to employ a few workers. Of the owners that I had met and spoken with, almost none desired to compete in larger markets. They were rooted in the community.

I realized that there was an unintended consequence to listening to speaker after speaker instruct conference participants about rapid business growth. It tempted me into believing that these small businesses were less-than, or somehow damaged. Of course, no one came out and said that. Instead, it was repeated over and over that the ideal is to be a bigger and more profitable entrepreneur. The small business, by its nature, serves as a foil to that goal.

Similarly, the way we speak about churches is predisposed against the small-membership church. When I ask denominational leaders about strong churches, they usually tell me about the largest congregations. When I ask about missional congregations, I usually hear about churches with multiple programs. These can easily become quantitative evaluations, rather than qualitative ones: more programs represent more vitality.

Though it might not be natural, our conversations about rural churches should also talk about their strength and their missional identities. This requires, of course, that we have a better understanding of both the congregations that we are discussing and what we mean when we use words like "vital," "strong," and "missional."

In the same way, congregations themselves should be careful about the words they use to describe themselves. When I talk to lay leaders, I often hear either a preemptive apologetic defense of their church, or I hear a downtrodden description. The first, the apologetic approach, is usually found with churches that sincerely want to be vital and strong. These churches are always quick to talk about how many ministries they have, how they have good members, and how active they are. The latter narrative is more negative. These are the churches that talk about their past numbers, lost youth, changes in society and culture, or the string of bad preachers.

Rather than overhype strengths or apologize for deficiencies, congregations can learn to talk about their particular strengths in ways that are both realistic and hopeful. One way to begin this is by using the indicators of vitality in chapter 2. How does the congregation see themselves as disciples of Christ? Where are they living that out in the community, either personally or as a congregation? How are they making the best uses of their resources?

This self-awareness makes for a better match between pastor and congregation. If the congregation is better able to articulate their real assets, as well as those areas where they are not as gifted, they are better situated to attract a pastor (either called or sent) that can provide meaningful leadership. Too, this self-awareness prevents the congregation from straying into either of the dominant narratives of failure or chaplaincy, as they are secure in their unique gifts.

Second, both congregations and denominational networks can increase their imaginations about what to do with failing congregations. Not every rural congregation will survive. Some congregations will simply die out. Some congregations will lose their will to keep going. Some will become insolvent.

In most instances, our options for these congregations seem to be either to close or hope for revitalization. Increasingly, there is also emphasis on creating a third avenue, such as repurposing property or mergers. There are valid reasons for all of these options, but these are not the limits of what is possible.

If churches are failing, careful attention needs to be paid to the local context before making a decision about closure. Denominations who are making the closure might consider forming a panel of local leaders to help consult about the significance of the congregation and the needs of the community. If the church is insolvent, but has a deep historical presence in the community, can the space be shared with another nonprofit? If we close the congregation, are we closing one of few community spaces? What will replace it? Are we providing for that replacement, so that we can continue to have a missional presence in this area? Establishing a panel of local leaders who are not congregation members to help think through the potential of the congregation and the space signifies a commitment to the community that will remain even if the congregation is gone, and opens up potential for more ministry with deeper contextuality.

Congregations, meanwhile, should continuously be thinking about their own organizational needs. Are they at a place where their resources would be best served by becoming having a bivocational or shared pastor? Are they adequately using their space, or is their space becoming a liability? What would be lost—both personally and communally—if the congregation were to disappear? What would be gained from a transformation into something new?

NEW MODELS OF RURAL MINISTRY

Rather than be locked in a binary choice between keeping small, rural churches open and closing them, the rural church can rethink their own structure in order to better utilize their resources and position themselves for community leadership. I want to briefly highlight three examples here, with a brief description of each, followed by some pros and cons. This is also not meant to be a lengthy discussion of these various models, but simple to explore a few options for models for maintaining a community presence where churches are no longer sustainable. An additional caveat is obvious: denominational structures and ecclesial polity will dictate the plausibility of these various models, and not all models will be suitable for every community.

Bivocational Ministry

A bivocational ministry, simply defined, is when the pastor has an additional job outside of the church that covers some or all of their living expenses. The immediate benefit, and the reason that many churches move to a bivocational model, is to reduce the cost of having a pastor to the congregation.

Bivocationality can take several different forms. I was briefly a bivocational pastor when I was appointed to a small parish while still finishing a yearlong fellowship to which I had committed. That bivocational period was short, lasting only about six months, while I transitioned into a full-time role as pastor. In other circumstances, pastors near a college or seminary might elect to have a part-time pastor who is also a student.

A bivocational pastor has a fulltime or part-time job outside of the congregation. At times, these jobs can closely align with their church ministry. For instance, some pastors secure positions that allow them to do missions and social work while serving as pastor. In my denomination, it is not unusual for those in regional leadership roles to serve as a bivocational pastor in an interim role. Or, a bivocational pastor might work for a parachurch organization. At other times, those roles are decidedly separate. A pastor might easily be a teacher, a small-business owner, a contractor, or any other number of professions.

There are some obvious assets here. As already mentioned, bivocational pastors usually provide some financial respite to the local parish where the pastor serves, particularly if the bulk of their salary is coming from their other vocation. Another key asset can be found in the experiences that the pastor brings in from their other positions. People who learn skills, like entrepreneurship and leadership, outside the walls of the church will be able to use those skills within the church. As Jason Byassee writes,

> Their entrepreneurial efforts are not a matter of multitasking; their efforts are not diffused. They have to concentrate to get good at what they're doing. Even though they're doing multiple things, they do them with Jesus' single eye.[7]

At times, these benefits are also tangible. When I moved to my pastorate, I brought with me a wide network of people who were interested in the leadership of the rural church. That network benefited my congregation and my community—we received grants to redo our website, we were awarded interns that we could not have afforded, and we had access to experts and educational opportunities to help us think about both missions and vitality.

Bivocational pastors also help parishioners reclaim a sense of vocation for themselves by offering a new vision for living out one's call. We learn from bivocational pastors that a calling can be lived out in creative and unique ways that merge all of your skills and passions. It does not have to be lived out in full-time ministry in the church; there are unlimited opportunities for being in ministry.

The last strength is perhaps the most notable. Bivocational pastors are grounded in the community in a way that few other pastors are. They remove the mystique of pastoral ministry and can identify with their parishioners about waking up to report to an office. They are serving their parishioners in their businesses, they are teaching students and interacting with parents, and they are leading nonprofits. All of this establishes deeper roots within the place they serve.

There are, of course, some areas where churches and pastors will need to exercise caution when moving to a bivocational model. The most significant is ensuring that both the church and pastor are comfortable with the amount of time the pastor is working within the church. If a church had a full-time pastor, they might become frustrated when the pastor is no longer readily available throughout the day, or when their other work has to be prioritized.

One way to make this transition from full-time pastor to bivocational pastor is to not think about the time in terms of when the pastor is on or off the clock. Instead, use this as an opportunity to reimage the pastoral role. How can the bivocational pastor help you live more into your role as an anchor institution? How does their dual role in the community strengthen the community more? What responsibilities, like some (but not all) aspects of pastoral care, can be led by the laity? What are the places where the pastor needs to focus their energy?

Mergers

Drive through any rural community, and you'll notice a plethora of small-membership churches. They dot the roadsides in the country; they sit on every street corner in small towns. Many are in the same denominational family: a series of small United Methodist Churches, all with less than twenty people within a short drive from each other, all next to a series of small Baptist churches, Pentecostal churches, and Presbyterian churches. This proliferation of churches made sense when the churches were founded, in the days when churchgoers traveled by foot and horseback. It makes less sense today, when cars make quick trips of several miles. All of this brings about the question: How do you realign these resources?

One solution has been to merge two or more churches into one new church. The benefits of this appear obvious, at first glance. If two or three churches have dwindling resources, by merging, they bolster their sustainability and heighten their impact in the community. By combining the expertise of their memberships, they can strengthen and expand their potential impact in the community.

While the potential of a merger seems obvious, it can be a challenging path. For starters, congregation members will need to recognize that there is a difference between *merger* and *acquisition.* In the latter, a larger body subsumes the smaller one. In an acquisition, the adaptation made by the larger church is one of welcoming and assimilating. But the adaptation made by the smaller entity is adjusting to a new culture. The end result in the acquisition is that the smaller entity is part of the larger one.

In a church merger, the two entities create a new, third entity. It is not simply taking the best practices from each congregation—it is deciding what makes the most sense for this new congregation. This can be hard for rural churches, which have long memories and deep traditions. Still, small-membership churches, which depend on relational leadership, are well suited to make this adaptation.

The two churches merging should not assume that the end result will be one church with a total of the combined average worship attendance, resources, or participation of two churches. Mergers will not magically double the worship attendance of the churches. In fact, when mergers are made for sustainability, the new church usually does not see a large boost in worship attendance.[8] In actuality, the worship attendance is often just the average of the two previous churches.[9]

Because of that, mergers should not be thought of as a quick way to grow a congregation, or as a surefire way to consolidate resources. Instead, church mergers need to be thought of as ways to facilitate a mission. If they are to happen, then all parties—the church members, pastoral leadership, and denominational leadership—need to be able to articulate a clear missional purpose on the front end. Leaders also need to communicate expectations of cultural shifts, constantly reminding the congregation that the end result will not be a summation of two parts, but a transformation into a new thing altogether.

Cooperative Realignments

Many churches might feel called to a partnership without the desire or missional reasoning to enter into a merger. For instance, imagine three churches that are all a short drive away from each other, but who serve three very different neighborhoods within the community. Each church is missionally present. One church hosts community events and offers meeting space their neighborhood. One distributes food for families that can't always go to the food bank in the center of the county. One provides a daycare, one of the few childcare facilities in the county.[10] A merger among these three entities might end up doing more community harm than good. Yet, financially, they would all benefit by sharing resources.

Two other realignments are open for churches in these situations. The first is purely cooperative model, reflecting equal ownership over the missional identity. Under this model, churches equally share (or proportionality share) the cost of staff. Costs for the overhead might be handled by each church on its own, or they might share costs across the network of two or more churches. By sharing a pastoral staff, though, the congregations are able to reduce their operating budget.

A cooperative model is more than just two churches sharing a staff. Though they might retain their individual worship life, the cooperative parish becomes missionally connected. Leadership about the future of the network is discussed by a leadership team of all the congregations. Missional strategies are set collectively. They hold a common identity, even as they retain some autonomy.

Similarly, adoption occurs when a smaller church is linked to a larger congregation. This is similar to establishing a satellite campus. In these instances, the pastor of the smaller church might share responsibilities as an associate pastor at the larger congregation. But the worship and social life of the church, like that of the cooperative parish model, might retain some autonomy. Or, they might offer a slightly different flavor of worship, with a modified sermon series based on what the larger church is offering, for instance.

There are multiple names for this kind of arrangement—daughter churches, adoption, multicampus, or hub and spoke. In rural communities, this type of arrangement is particularly helpful when the county-seat church is vital and can share missional strategies with smaller churches in the surrounding, more remote areas. The stronger missional presence of the county-seat church gives an opportunity for the smaller congregation to join in the work of being an anchor institution with an established presence. And it gives the larger church the ability to reach further out into the community.

Both of these mean some change for all of the congregations involved. In some instances, they might be able to retain much of their existing congregational culture. But they will also have to learn to participate and cooperate in the wider network. For churches that are moving into hub-and-spoke congregational models, the smaller churches will necessarily have to come to terms with accepting leadership from the mother church. This may mean relaunching the congregation with a new missional focus.

One example of this is Hayesville First United Methodist Church in Western North Carolina. The county-seat church has a strong community presence and a robust congregational life. When a smaller congregation closed, Hayesville First acquired the property and relaunched it as the Sweetwater Campus. On Saturday nights, they hold The Bridge, a meal and worship service that is designed and focused on addiction recovery. This new worship service, which was born out of existing recovery ministries, was formed in part as a response to the opioid crisis facing rural communities in the United States.[11]

While this relaunch is treated as a new church, the hub-and-spoke model can be highly adaptable, depending on the congregations involved. Regardless, establishing these sorts of cooperative networks requires a great deal of intentionality, with missional priorities leading the conversation.

CREATING ACCOUNTABILITY

A significant part of this book has focused on the narratives that others tell about rural communities and congregations. It's important to highlight these narratives because churches tend to believe them, to occupy them, and to form themselves around them. When the story that people hear about themselves is negative, eventually, that becomes the narrative that people live into.

A friend of mine pastored a small-membership church in a small town. A few years before he became the pastor, a well-intentioned regional leader told them they had about five years before they would be closed, if nothing changed. I suspect that the leader wanted to shock them into changing or growing. That is a common enough tactic, after all. If the church is shocked into thinking they will close, they will be spurred to action. By creating the narrative of necessity, the regional leader wanted to foster innovation. It's not unlike telling a student that unless they buckle down and learn to study, they will fail.

The challenge, of course, is that when a student never knew they were failing, or when they were absolutely doing the best they could, then the student is baffled and afraid to learn that they are in danger of not passing. Rather than convincing the student to try harder, they might only convince the student to give up. After all, if they were already doing their best and it wasn't working, then they reason that they themselves are actually failures.

This was, unfortunately, what happened in my friend's church. When he arrived, a couple of years after that tough-love treatment had been given, the church was mentally prepared to close. Instead of believing they could do more, they believed that nothing would work. Each time my friend sought to bring out a new initiative or to launch a new mission, the church would reject the proposal.

"What's the point?" they asked. "Two years ago, they told us we have five years left. Now we're down to three."

My friend's ministry to that church became one of undoing the damage of well-meaning church-growth experts: convincing the church that the promise of resurrection was still true, even for them. He had the gargantuan task of undoing the narrative written by those who had castigated the church for resisting various church growth tactics and strategies.

Narratives matter, and my sincerest hope is that the narrative around the rural church will shift to see the potential and promise of rural communities. It would be a folly, though, for churches to assume that the wider narrative will change without their action. Rather than wait for the narrative to change, the rural church must be the one to rewrite the broader narrative.

The immediate task before the rural church is to put in place structures of accountability that make that shift possible. The accountability that we are talking about here is twofold. First, the local church must own that they are responsible for articulating a theological and communal vision for their context. There is no way that these accountability structures can be crafted from outside of the organization. These are necessarily internal.

Second, these goals need to be grounded in a few different places. They must account for the vitality of the congregation, yes. But they must also account for the evangelical and theological convictions of the congregation. Lastly, they must be subjected to constant evaluation, as practice and reflection offer new insights.

A basic structure of this accountability begins with an examination of vitality found in chapter 2. Readers will remember that within this structure of vitality, there are three indicators: theological identity, commitment to community, and stewardship of resources. These areas provide a place for churches to think through who they are as an organization.

The basic questions, then, are not so much on theoretical concepts, but rather questions of *how*. As churches emphasize a theological identity, the rural church should begin with a series of questions: How you will deepen the sense of vocation and theological identity of the congregation? What practices need to be instituted? Is that a change in preaching? New Bible studies? How will the voices of the congregation inform how those changes are made?

Likewise, for increasing community commitment, the questions should revolve around how the congregation understands itself in light of the community: How do we get to know our neighbors, on their terms? How do we find where people are gathering? How do we become more integrated into the life of this community? How do we meet specific needs?

Lastly, churches should evaluate their own stewardship. How are we utilizing the resources of this group? How could we better use that money, time, or talent? How does our organizational structure waste our resources? How could we be better organized to carry out a mission?

As churches grow in their own organizational capacity, they should then begin thinking about accountability to their evangelism. Here, congregations might simply choose to walk through the fourfold model of evangelism presented in chapter 3. Where do we recognize the Kingdom of God, both in ourselves and in the community? How are we cultivating that presence? How is our work announcing God's Kingdom, and how do we understand our own actions in light of God's Kingdom? How can we invite others to participate in this kingdom, by helping others understand these practices and begin to embody these means of grace?

This, necessarily, requires persistent theological reflection. Is our commitment to community one of charity? Or is it one of justice? To which are we being called at this moment in our journey? Are we providing basic needs, or are we forming deeper relationships with our community? And are we rooted in our vision of what the Kingdom of God is, or are we simply offering another service, like other nonprofits?

Congregations will likely find that the answers to these questions, if they are being faithful in asking and reflecting, will ultimately shape how they respond to answers in another area of their church life. As the church lives into its role as an anchor institution, then they will no doubt reorient their understanding of their commitment to community. In turn, that will shift the resources that they recognize and utilize, which will in turn shape their calling to justice, relationships, and solidarity.

This is in itself a practice of sanctification, a process of becoming perfected over time. When establishing these practices of accountability, then, churches need to remember a few important ideas.

First, there is no silver bullet. The practice of forming disciples is a long one. The process of leading community is a complex one. The task of learning more about God is a never-ending one. It is beyond our ability to predict every variable, or to know how God will change our communities.

Second, accountability requires congregations to commit themselves to particular values, rather than aimlessly jump from strategy to strategy. By grounding themselves, they will be able to keep on a course, confident in their identity and able to navigate whatever shifting landscape they face.

Third, and relatedly, churches need to be reflective. While values should not be abandoned, practices can always be modified and tweaked over the long term. When I began learning to play musical instruments, my teachers would teach me fundamental techniques, like how to hold the instrument, where to place my hands, and how to read music. Most importantly, my teachers taught me how to count. We began, of course, with a simple 4/4 standard beat, and I would tap my foot along to the quarter notes and half notes, dutifully counting in my head with the metronome. Over time, the music would become harder. At first, it was small transitions, like learning to count in 3/4 time instead of 4/4. Then it got harder. I learned to count in 6/8, for instance. Later, the music we played would change time signatures multiple times in the same piece—I learned how to change my counting so that I could play and understand the beauty of the music.

The journey of sanctification is not unlike learning to play an instrument. We learn certain fundamentals that are nonnegotiable. But as we grow in our abilities, we necessarily learn to pivot, to adapt, and to do more complex things. We learn that, while it's always important to count, we might find ourselves counting in new ways. Sometimes we count a simple beat. Sometimes the beat is obscure. Sometimes it changes frequently. Nevertheless, we constantly rely on the fundamentals that we learned.

Our goal, as John Wesley reminded his followers, is Christian Perfection. That is decidedly not our starting point. As churches learn to establish their own practices of accountability, they will also learn that they will continuously be reexamining these practices. They will be constantly adapting and learning more about themselves as they grow closer to God. As they help others see the Kingdom of God around them, they will learn to see more of God's Kingdom for themselves. This is an integral part of the Christian journey.

THE FUTURE OF THE RURAL CHURCH

A few weeks after I started in my current position, I asked my boss, our college president, a naive question, one that I should have asked during the job interview. I had read about a small college closing, and I was suddenly very afraid that our college was on that trajectory. We were driving in a car on the way home from a fundraising trip, and we had a few hours to kill.

"We're not like other small colleges facing uncertainty, are we?"

My boss didn't even glance at me. "Almost every small college has challenges," he said. "You can be afraid of that, or you can see it as an opportunity to lead."

I'm afraid that for a long time we've viewed rural churches as places where fear dominates. We are afraid that they are unable to change, we are afraid to tamper with those qualities that make them deeply loved, or we are afraid to explore the counterintuitive strengths of small churches.

It's worth mentioning, though, that the spread of Christianity is the result of small-membership churches. Consider, for instance, one of the major contributors to the religious formation in the United States during the eighteenth and nineteenth centuries. The noted historian Nathan Hatch reminds us that between 1776 and 1850, Methodists grew from less than 3 percent of church members to more than 34 percent. Hatch attributes this, in part, to Methodism's growth in the "American backcountry."[12] This backcountry religion inspired a great deal of social change: it was responsible for bridging ethnic and language barriers, overcoming class barriers, empowering local religious music, and cultivating social mobility by giving members vocations to be preachers, local pastors, class leaders, and traveling elders. These Methodists founded colleges and schools, making education accessible for many parts of rural America.

What is striking about this early Methodist movement is that it intentionally sought out the rural periphery. It was an integral part of its DNA, embedded in the structure of the organization's purpose. As Hatch writes,

> Most Congregational ministers, educated at Yale, Harvard, and Dartmouth, simple chose to remain and serve congregations in "civilized" areas. While Methodism retained a stronghold in the seaports of the middle states, [Francis] Asbury hammered its organization into one that had a distinct rural orientation, adept at expanding into thinly populated areas. "We must draw resources from the centre to the circumference," Asbury wrote in 1794.[13]

The spread of Methodism in the United States was not in spite of its rural nature; it was because of it. Its emphasis on creating small chapels all around allowed it a great degree of adaptability, and to intimately become part of its members' lives. It was not fancy or culturally prestigious, but it was transformational nonetheless, as people habituated themselves into the Christian faith, and in turn fundamentally transforming communities for the better.

Critics of small-membership and rural churches will point out, rightfully, that the proportion between rural populations and urban populations is substantially different now than it was in the eighteenth and nineteenth century. They will note that most people live in suburban and urban areas, and that our emphasis should be on lifting up these churches.

They are not wrong about the shifts in population, but those who would call us to abandon or shutter rural churches because they are rural and small miss an important point. In rural places, these churches are part of a legacy of transformation and evangelism that needs to be remembered and relived. These legacies have a great deal to teach us about the potential of the church to bring about the Kingdom of God.

More than that, these communities are beacons of hope in communities that face unique challenges. While it is not true that rural communities are wholesale collapsing, or that every rural community is a place of despair and decay, it is fair to say that rural communities do face some difficulties. Recovery after the Great Recession took much longer than it did for urban and suburban communities.[14] It would be disingenuous for anyone to say that rural communities face no challenges. As I write, the entire globe is facing the COVID19 pandemic. Already lagging in medical infrastructure, and with most rural counties having narrowly focused economies, rural communities will most certainly face a challenging recovery.[15]

As some of the few permanent anchor institutions in their communities, rural congregations are well poised to offer leadership. More so, they have a responsibility to be leaders. For denominations, rural congregations represent an opportunity to revitalize their own missions in these areas, and lay claim to a profound heritage that, historically, sparked major religious movements in the United States.

For the rural church, this is an opportunity to reclaim a narrative about their own identity. Rural churches can retell their own story, holding up the important work they do in not only strengthening their communities, but in reaffirming the importance of evangelism and discipleship formation. It's an opportunity for the rural church to exercise the unique strengths they have as deeply relational people, as integrated into the community, and as trusted institutions to create meaningful change. Most of all, it's an opportunity for the rural church to lead transformation that helps live into the words of the prayer that gets spoken each week: *Your kingdom come, Your will be done on earth as it is in heaven.*

It is not easy work, and I do not want churches to believe that it is. But the journey of discipleship is not meant to be easy; there is a reason that Christ relates it to carrying a cross. I will also maintain that not every rural church will be able to adjust or live into the process of evangelism and vitality outlined here. As I have tried to make clear, there are churches that have reached the limits of their lifespan. There are churches that are tired and worn out, members who struggle to keep the small institution afloat out of a sense of duty. For those congregations, there should be some permission to let go.

Pastors, meanwhile, should not naturally expect that every church will immediately want to join in the work outlined here. Again, this is a process that mirrors and draws from a journey toward sanctification. Part of the role of a pastor is not to expect that their parishioners have already reached sanctification, but to assume that they are on that journey together. The role of a pastor is many things, but it is also one of a coach and encourager.

An underlying emphasis on this book has been the importance of community to the leadership of the rural church, whether in articulating vitality, leading community transformation, or perfecting practices. Church leaders will need to seek out, listen to, and understand the voices of their congregations, even when those voices are resistant. This work cannot be done alone. A single member cannot name all of the assets. A single church by itself does not make a partnership. An individual does not constitute a community.

For rural congregations, the journey to reclaiming the vitality and evangelistic spirit that is innate within might be a long one. But it is possible, if it is properly grounded and directed toward revealing the Kingdom of God. The rural church does not have to fit neatly into a narrative of romanticized community or decline and decay. The rural church does not have to twist itself into inadequate standards of vitality, or abandon its practices of evangelism and mission.

Instead, the rural church can lay claim to their unique strengths and resiliency. They can reorient their understanding of vitality, cultivating increased faithfulness in their own contexts. They can recognize, cultivate, announce, and invite their community to participate in the Kingdom that God has already established, and be a formational and transformational leader. The rural church does not have to live by the narrative that others create for it. They can reclaim their identity, their discipleship, and their mission. They can reclaim the gift of being a rural church.

NOTES

1. Deasy, Jo Anne. "What Do Seminary Graduates Want to Do with Their Degrees?" *Trust* 30, no. 3 (2019): 20–21.

2. "Elaine A. Heath: God's People, Gathered, Blessed and Sent Out." '*Faith and Leadership*, April 5, 2016, faithandleadership.com/elaine-heath-gods-people-gathered-blessed-and-sent-out.

3. Pao, Maureen. "At U.S. Seminaries, A Rise In Millennials Answering God's Call." *NPR*, September 23, 2015, www.npr.org/2015/09/23/442243849/at-u-s-seminaries-a-rise-in-millennials-answering-gods-call.

4. Tisdale, Leonora Tubbs. *Preaching as Local Theology and Folk Art.* Fortress Press, 2010. 23.

5. Kotan and Schroeder, *Small Church Checkup'*. Kotan and Schroeder argue in chapter 7 that this is a role that many churches play.

6. Parks, Lewis. *Small on Purpose: Life in a Significant Church.* Abingdon Press, 2017.

7. Byassee, Jason. "Jason Byassee: We May All Be Headed to Bivocational Ministry." Future Pastors May All Need to Be Bivocational Ministers | By Jason Byassee | Faith & Leadership, June 3, 2013, faithandleadership.com/jason-byassee-we-may-all-be-headed-bivocational-ministry.

8. Walker, Ken. "Let's Get Together: Most Mergers Driven by Mission, Not Survival." *Christianity Today*, September 9, 2011, 14.

9. Stanton, Allen. "Interview on Church Mergers with Western North Carolina Annual Conference Legacy Initiative." February 14, 2019.

10. A lack of access to childcare is well-noted in rural areas, with significant economic impacts. For one study, see Henning-Smith, Carrie, and Katy B. Kozhimannil. "Availability of Child Care in Rural Communities: Implications for Workforce Recruitment and Retention." *Journal of Community Health* 41, no. 3 (2015): 488–93, doi:10.1007/s10900-015-0120-3.

11. "About." *The Bridge*, www.thebridgehayesville.org/about.html.

12. Hatch, Nathan O. "The Puzzle of American Methodism." *Church History* 63, no. 2 (1994): 175–89, doi:10.2307/3168586.

13. Ibid.

14. This is a widely recognized truth, but for one analysis, see Cohen, Norma. "Financial Times 'Rural America' Slow to Recover." *Financial Times*, November 11, 2013, www.ft.com/content/8326d14e-4aed-11e3-8c4c-00144feabdc0.

15. Monnat, Shannon. "Research Update: Why Coronavirus Could Hit Rural Areas Harder." *Daily Yonder*, March 24, 2020, www.dailyyonder.com/research-update-why-coronavirus-could-hit-rural-areas-harder/2020/03/24/.

Bibliography

Aamot, Gregg. "Nonprofits, Mirroring a National Trend, Grow in Minnesota's Smallest Places," August 28, 2015. http://www.minnpost.com/rural-dispatches /2015/08/nonprofits-mirroring-national-trend-grow-minnesota-s-smallest-places/.

Abraham, William J. *The Logic of Evangelism*. Grand Rapids, MI: Eerdmans, 2006.

Arias, Mortimer. *Announcing the Reign of God: Evangelization and the Subversive Memory of Jesus*. Lima, OH: Academic Renewal Press, 1984.

Benedict XVI. "Deus Caritas Est (December 25, 2005): BENEDICT XVI," December 24, 2005. http://www.vatican.va/content/benedict-xvi/en/encyclicals/documents/hf _ben-xvi_enc_20051225_deus-caritas-est.html.

Berry, Wendell. *Jayber Crow: The Life Story of Jayber Crow, Barber, of the Port William Membership, as Written by Himself*. Thorndike, ME: Thorndike Press, 2001.

Berry, Wendell. *What Matters?: Economics for a Renewed Commonwealth*. Berkeley, CA: Counterpoint, 2010.

Brice-Saddler, Michael. "A Wealthy Televangelist Explains His Fleet of Private Jets: 'It's a Biblical Thing'," June 4, 2019. https://www.washingtonpost.com/religion/ 2019/06/04/wealthy-televangelist-explains-his-fleet-private-jets-its-biblical-thing/.

Brooks, David. "What Rural America Has to Teach Us," March 21, 2019. https://ww w.nytimes.com/2019/03/21/opinion/nebraska-rural-america.html.

Brown, Jeffrey, and Mike Fritz. "Why Millennials Are Moving Away from Large Urban Centers," December 2, 2019. http://www.pbs.org/newshour/show/why-mil lennials-are-moving-away-from-large-urban-centers.

Byassee, Jason. "Jason Byassee: We May All Be Headed to Bivocational Ministry," June 3, 2013. https://faithandleadership.com/jason-byassee-we-may-all-be-headed -bivocational-ministry.

Byassee, Jason. *The Gifts of the Small Church*. Nashville, TN: Abingdon Press, 2010.

Candid. "More Millennials Value Volunteering Than Previous Generation Did," January 5, 2015. http://philanthropynewsdigest.org/news/more-millennials-value -volunteering-than-previous-generation-did.

Catte, Elizabeth. *What You Are Getting Wrong about Appalachia*. Cleveland, OH: Belt Publishing, 2018.

Collaborative for Neighborhood Transformation. "ABCD Toolkit: What Is Asset Based Community Development?" Accessed 2020. https://resources.depaul.edu/abcd-instit ute/resources/Documents/WhatisAssetBasedCommunityDevelopment.pdf.

Connerton, Paul. *How Societies Remember*. Cambridge: Cambridge University Press, 1989.

Cromartie, John, and Shawn Bucholtz. "Defining the 'Rural' in Rural America," June 1, 2008. https://www.ers.usda.gov/amber-waves/2008/june/defining-the-rural-in-r ural-america/.

Danbom, David B. *Born in the Country a History of Rural America*. Baltimore, MD: Johns Hopkins University Press, 2017.

Deasy, Jo Anne. "What Do Seminary Graduates Want to Do with Their Degrees?" *In Trust* 30, no. 3 (2019): 20–21.

De Wetter, Davide, Ilene Gochman, Rich Luss, and Rick Sherwood. "United Methodist Church Call To Action: Vital Congregation Research Project." Nashville, TN: United Methodist Church, 2010.

Dierdorff, Jonathan. Interview with Jonathan Dierdorff. Personal, March 3, 2020.

Dudley, Carl S. *Effective Small Churches in the Twenty-First Century*. Nashville, TN: Abingdon Press, 2003.

Ebrahim, Alnoor. *The Many Faces of Nonprofit Accountability*. Cambridge, MA: Harvard Business School, 2010.

Fischbeck, Lisa G. "Lisa G. Fischbeck: The Strength and Beauty of Small Churches," July 15, 2013. https://faithandleadership.com/lisa-g-fischbeck-strength-and-beau ty-small-churches.

Goetz, Stephan J., Mark D. Partridge, and Heather M. Stephens. "The Economic Status of Rural America in the President Trump Era and Beyond." *Applied Economic Perspectives and Policy* 40, no. 1 (2018): 97–118. https://doi.org/10 .1093/aepp/ppx061.

Harkins, Anthony, and Meredith McCarroll. *Appalachian Reckoning a Region Responds to Hillbilly Elegy*. Morgantown, WV: West Virginia University Press, 2019.

Hart, Trevor A. *Between the Image and the Word: Theological Engagements with Imagination, Language and Literature*. New York, NY: Routledge, 2016.

Hatch, Nathan O. "The Puzzle of American Methodism." *Church History* 63, no. 2 (1994): 175–89. https://doi.org/10.2307/3168586.

Heath, Elaine A. *The Mystic Way of Evangelism: A Contemplative Vision for Christian Outreach*. Grand Rapids, MI: Baker Academic, 2008.

Heath, Elaine. "Elaine A. Heath: God's People, Gathered, Blessed and Sent Out," April 5, 2016. https://faithandleadership.com/elaine-heath-gods-people-gathered- blessed-and-sent-out.

Henning-Smith, Carrie, and Katy B. Kozhimannil. "Availability of Child Care in Rural Communities: Implications for Workforce Recruitment and Retention." *Journal of Community Health* 41, no. 3 (2015): 488–93. https://doi.org/10.1007/s 10900-015-0120-3.

House, Silas. "Eastern Kentucky Has Been Underwater, but You Probably Didn't Notice," February 23, 2020. https://www.theatlantic.com/ideas/archive/2020/02/eastern-kentucky-is-underwater-but-you-probably-didnt-notice/606973/.

Knight, Henry H., and F. Douglas Powe. *Transforming Evangelism: The Wesleyan Way of Sharing Faith.* Nashville, TN: Discipleship Resources, 2013.

Kuja, Ryan. *From the Inside Out: Reimagining Mission, Recreating the World.* Eugene, OR: Cascade Books, 2018.

Lacy, Bridgette A. "A Community Grows Its Way Out of Poverty," October 6, 2015. https://faithandleadership.com/community-grows-its-way-out-poverty.

Long, D. Stephen. *Divine Economy Theology and the Market.* London: Taylor and Francis, 2002.

Maddox, Randy L. *Responsible Grace: John Wesley's Practical Theology.* Nashville, TN: Kingswood Books, 1994.

Meserole, W. H. "What Do You Mean: Rural and Urban?" *Journal of Marketing* 2, no. 3 (1938): 233. https://doi.org/10.2307/1246386.

Monnat, Shannon. "Research Update: Why Coronavirus Could Hit Rural Areas Harder," June 2, 2020. http://www.dailyyonder.com/research-update-why-coronavirus-could-hit-rural-areas-harder/2020/03/24/.

Newport, Frank. "Americans Big on Idea of Living in the Country," April 8, 2020. https://news.gallup.com/poll/245249/americans-big-idea-living-country.aspx.

Newport, Frank. "Americans Big on Idea of Living in the Country," December 7, 2019. https://news.gallup.com/poll/245249/americans-big-idea-living-country.aspx.

Pao, Maureen. "At U.S. Seminaries, A Rise in Millennials Answering God's Call," September 23, 2015. http://www.npr.org/2015/09/23/442243849/at-u-s-seminaries-a-rise-in-millennials-answering-gods-call.

Parks, Lewis. *Small on Purpose: Life in a Significant Church.* Nashville, TN: Abingdon Press, 2017.

Porter, Eduardo. "The Hard Truths of Trying to 'Save' the Rural Economy," December 14, 2018. https://www.nytimes.com/interactive/2018/12/14/opinion/rural-america-trump-decline.html.

Rendle, Gilbert R. *Doing the Math of Mission: Fruits, Faithfulness, and Metrics.* Lanham, MD: Rowman & Littlefield, 2014.

Rendle, Gilbert R. *Quietly Courageous: Leading the Church in a Changing World.* Lanham, MD: Rowman & Littlefield, an imprint of The Rowman & Littlefield Publishing Group, Inc., 2019.

Rieger, Joerg. *No Rising Tide: Theology, Economics, and the Future.* Minneapolis, MN: Fortress Press, 2009.

Rieger, Joerg, and Pui-lan Kwok. *Occupy Religion: Theology of the Multitude.* Lanham, MD: Rowman & Littlefield, 2013.

Riney-Kehrberg, Pamela. *The Routledge History of Rural America.* New York, NY: Routledge Taylor & Francis Group, 2017.

Schroeder, Phil, and Kay Kotan. *Small Church Checkup: Assessing Your Church's Health and Creating a Treatment Plan.* Nashville, TN: Discipleship Resources, 2018.

Senior, John E. *A Theology of Political Vocation: Christian Life and Public Office.* Waco, TX: Baylor University Press, 2015.

Skinner, Jennifer. "If There's Another Flood, 'I Certainly Won't Wait for Anybody to Call Me. I'll Just Come Down, Start Paddling'," September 27, 2017. https://www.100daysinappalachia.com/2017/06/rainelle-flood-2016-resucers-remember/.

Stanton, Allen. Interview on Church Mergers with Western North Carolina Annual Conference Legacy Initiative. Personal, February 14, 2019.

Stone, Bryan P. *Evangelism after Christendom: The Theology and Practice of Christian Witness.* Grand Rapids, MI: Baker Pub. Group, 2007.

Swenson, David. "Most of America's Rural Areas Are Doomed to Decline," July 8, 2019. https://theconversation.com/most-of-americas-rural-areas-are-doomed-to-decline-115343?utm_medium=email.

Theodori, Gene L. "Community and Community Development in Resource-Based Areas: Operational Definitions Rooted in an Interactional Perspective." *Society & Natural Resources* 18, no. 7 (2005): 661–69. https://doi.org/10.1080/08941920590959640.

Tisdale, Leonora Tubbs. *Preaching as Local Theology and Folk Art.* Minneapolis, MN: Fortress Press, 2010.

Toner, Kathleen. "'By Nourishing Plants, You're Nourishing Community'," March 21, 2016. http://www.cnn.com/2015/09/24/us/cnn-heroes-joyner/index.html.

Vance, J. D. *Hillbilly Elegy.* New York, NY: HarperCollins Books, 2016.

Walker, Ken. "Let's Get Together: Most Mergers Driven by Mission, Not Survival." *Christianity Today*, September 9, 2011.

Warner, Laceye C. *Saving Women: Retrieving Evangelistic Theology and Practice.* Waco, TX: Baylor University Press, 2007.

Weber, Bruce, J. Matthew Fannin, Kathleen Miller, and Stephan Goetz. "Intergenerational Mobility of Low-Income Youth in Metropolitan and Non-Metropolitan America: A Spatial Analysis." *Regional Science Policy & Practice* 10, no. 2 (2018): 87–101. https://doi.org/10.1111/rsp3.12122.

Wells, Samuel. *Nazareth Manifesto.* Chichester: Wiley-Blackwell, 2015.

Wesley, John, Albert C. Outler, and Richard P. Heitzenrater. *John Wesley's Sermons: An Anthology.* Nashville, TN: Abingdon Press, 1991.

Index

About the Author

Allen T. Stanton is the executive director of the Turner Center at Martin Methodist College and an ordained minister in The United Methodist Church. Previously, he has served as the pastor of a small-membership rural church in North Carolina, and as the Rural Faith Communities Fellow at the Institute for Emerging Issues, a public policy think tank at North Carolina State University.

Allen holds degrees from Wake Forest University and Duke Divinity School. At Duke Divinity, Allen was both a Thriving Rural Communities Fellow and the Center for Reconciliation's World Vision Justice Fellow. Allen frequently writes, speaks, and leads workshops on rural ministry and community development. To learn more about his work, visit www.cultivaterural.com.